THE PRODIGAL, SON'S PRODIGAL FATHER

RICHARD MAUTHE

PAGE PUBLISHING
Conneaut Lake, PA

First originally published by Page Publishing 2024

ISBN 979-8-89315-970-7 (pbk)
ISBN 979-8-89315-985-1 (digital)

Printed in the United States of America

To my wife, Edith, with love.

CONTENTS

*But there are also many other things that Jesus did;
if every one of them were written down, I suppose that the world
itself could not contain the books that would be written.*

—John 21:25

I suppose John had me in mind when he wrote these words to conclude the Gospel account. Or maybe not. What I do know is that God's action in Jesus of Nazareth is the most critical event in what has proven to be the sad story of humanity apart from God. For almost two thousand years now, the world, then and now, has struggled to understand exactly who Jesus is, what importance he has for *all* of humanity and the creation, and perhaps most critically, how each and every person responds to his probing question: "*But who do you say that I am*" (Matthew 16:15)?

The Christian Church has been used and abused by secular forces since day one, it seems, and even the Church has, sadly enough, imposed its own understanding of God on peoples and nations—sometimes out of good intentions, at other times because of heads swollen with power and authority. Today's backlash against institutionalized Christianity, mostly in the Western world, still does not diminish the importance of Jesus of Nazareth for every generation of believer and nonbeliever. This is why I am adding my own understanding of the Man from Nazareth, as my thoughts reflect, to a great extent, the age in which I find myself. Of course, I fully expect pearl clutchers to dispute much of what follows; that is okay because I know my worth is not in what I do or write but in whose I am.

So my hope is that laypersons who struggle in reconciling opposing, confusing, and conflicting views of God and who find many passages of Scripture downright strange and contradictory will come to recognize certain threads that are apparent (well, sometimes well hidden) throughout the Hebrew and Christian testaments.

However we recognize these threads, they all lead not to a point bound to time and place but to the God of unfathomable love, who loves the creation—of which we are, each and every one of us—a minute part. That God loves a creature who is so fallible, so unsure of itself, whose time is fleeting, is the message we all need to struggle with and take into our hearts.

INTRODUCTION

I was accosted in my own backyard by an individual who sought me out and went on a rant about God and how God was punishing the United States because of the then-present circumstances. This was just a few years ago, when COVID-19 was just beginning its stranglehold on society. I understand tempers were short, frustration was long, and folks were looking for someone, anyone, to blame.

This person is a professed Christian and yet went into an absolute tirade about the just desserts we were experiencing, all of it the judgment of God upon the United States because of gay marriage, abortion, and a few other hot-button social issues.

Well, rant over, the individual abruptly turned on his heels and walked away. I was somewhat shell-shocked and made my way back into the safety of my house. I began to ruminate about how the story of a God of unconditional love could be dragged into such an unloving monologue—a deliberate, respectful, mutual conversation it was not.

So…how *does* one reconcile the God we have come to know and love in Jesus of Nazareth with a raging Old Testament God, who is just waiting to lower the boom on yet another generation of wayward kids? How *does* one reconcile Old Testament episodes of brutal ethnic cleansing with the Son of God, who welcomed foreigners, sinners, and outcasts without exception, into the immediacy of the Kingdom of God?

What helps me in my own teaching and preaching and interactions with folks is remembering the real purpose of our being part of God's called people: that we are to be a blessing to others so that the recipients of our blessings come to acknowledge and worship the God of Israel as the source of life and a constant help in times of trouble—not through a whirlwind descent from heaven, smiting the enemy, but rather through the sometimes gentle, sometimes brash structures of society and through those individuals who reach out to us in our own times of need.

This does not mean cherry-picking chapters and verses that support or contrast with any "liberal" interpretation of Scripture but rather keeping in mind the overarching call to God's people, be they in biblical times or our own.

It also reminds us who struggle with Scripture to remember the *Sitz im Leben*—what was happening in the lives of the people at that time, and how did they interpret the tragedies and crises that came, then as now, on a regular basis?

My approach is to keep in mind that the Scriptures are, indeed, inerrant—in matters of the gospel, which is not limited to the pages of the New Testament. God coming to God's people in every era, then and now, is something to be celebrated and brought to bear upon a suffering humanity.

> *And ye, beneath life's crushing load,*
> *Whose forms are bending low,*
> *Who toil along the climbing way*
> *With painful steps and slow:*
> *Look now! for glad and golden hours*
> *Come swiftly on the wing;*
> *O rest beside the weary road,*
> *And hear the angels sing.* ("It Came Upon the Midnight Clear")

I suspect this verse of "*It Came upon a Midnight Clear*" doesn't resonate very well with those expecting relief from "life's crushing load" on Christmas Eve, and here we are singing about it! But if life were just a Hallmark movie, we wouldn't need divine intervention to rescue us. It's just that ascribing to God what Jesus didn't ascribe to God adds to the crushing load, as it drives people away from God.

I recently ran into a European, who excoriated Christianity today because of…the Crusades. The Crusades.

Perhaps, just perhaps, what we like to ascribe to "divine retribution" is our feeling the consequences of our own actions, whether dumb, intentional, or not intentional. Perhaps, just perhaps, ancient Israel saw divine retribution in the consequences of their adultery due to their syncretism (the blending of differing religions, in this case) with surrounding pagan religions, damaging the marital relationship with Yahweh, but never beyond hope and restoration. Perhaps we are ascribing to God humanity's penchant for being fed up, disgusted with, and focusing on a vengeance- and retribution-oriented approach to life.

Perhaps if we just let go of those descriptions of God, we are not left with a hollowed-out deity who is not concerned about justice, about the existence of hatred, prejudice, social injustice, unfairness, and the like. But is perhaps a deity who, in Jesus, conquered even the last enemy, death, by love.

Perhaps then we are called to reclaim that which often has been stolen from the church or ignored by it—a truly *evangelical* faith grounded in the gospel and not seduced by the culture wars so noisy and overwhelming in not just this particular era but that arise in every age. *"We must obey God rather than any human authority"* has been true since Peter and the apostles said these words in Acts 5:29. Christianity in the early decades of the twenty-first century is at yet another crossroad, especially in the northern hemisphere. Will we live out the welcoming good news, in which the alien is embraced, the downtrodden cared for, the vulnerable protected, the legions of hungry fed in countries where being overweight is becoming the norm? Or will we head in the direction of legislating morality? Because a legalistic take on both the Hebrew and Christian scriptures lead just to that: a legalistic interpretation of the good news of Jesus and a hammering of those who are different. But God calls us to live as new creatures, a gift given to followers of Jesus, resurrection in this life.

This brief text is not about reclaiming the gospel—the gospel is in and of itself free; it cannot be constrained by human attempts. Rather, we are called to make its blessed truth part of our raison d'être in how we respond to God in the person of the neighbor, be that neighbor a spouse, an extended family member, weird kid on the block, or the nation. This is an attempt to clarify, uncover, resee with a new different understanding, the mystery of God, the strange righteousness of God that God is pleased to grant us all for the sake of Jesus, our Lord and Savior.

PART 1

UNREQUITED LOVE

My spouse's favorite flower is the gardenia. For decades now I have grown at least one plant in the colder northeast in a pot to be moved inside in cooler weather here in Arizona, outside 24-7. It is the fragrance of the gardenia which makes it so special to both of us. How does one describe that, though? I might say, somewhat like a rose scent but spicier. I am working from the known to the unknown in providing a point of reference to offer another person a helpful connection to the scent. Which is unique to the plant and which description can only approximate what one experiences. So a rose remains a rose, a gardenia remains a gardenia; they aren't the same, but the novice plant lover might make a connection.

So it is with the familiar stories of the Bible, especially those of the New Testament. Over the millennia, even the writers of the Bible have used familiar known images and concepts of their faith to help bridge the gap of God's mystery in Jesus and have drawn into the conversation the common religious symbols, beliefs, and theologies people of that day and age understood.

As an example, one might connect Jesus to the story of the "Sacrifice of Issac" in Genesis because of the language and imagery used. How can we make that claim? In Matthew 3:17, God speaks

1

from heaven at the Baptism: "This is my Son, the Beloved, with whom I am well pleased." In Genesis 22:2, God speaks to Abraham: "Take your son, your only son, Isaac, whom you love, and go to the land of Moriah." In the LXX (The Septuagint, the Greek translation of the Hebrew Bible), God describes Isaac as ὁ υἱός ἀγαπήτος (the son, [the] beloved). In Matthew, Jesus is described as ὁ υἱός μου ἀγαπήτος (the son of me, [the] beloved). While somewhat subtle in English, the connection is more forceful in Greek, and Jesus is identified with, and becomes, the Lamb of God who takes away the sin of the world. So words of sacrifice, sacrificial lamb, atonement, and others—well understood by then believers—become standard ways of describing God's saving action in Jesus, especially during the Season of Lent.

But at what price for God? God becomes for many people a God seeking a blood sacrifice to make up the failure of the human race to redeem itself in God's eyes. God then becomes a never-satisfied deity, who is constantly frowning, arms crossed, either waiting for us to make yet another mistake in our lives or who will check up on St. Peter's admissions through the Pearly Gates and review the list of failures we make. True or not? In conducting almost five hundred funerals in my pastoral career, in the vast majority of family visitation before and after the funeral, some comment was made pointing out the insecurity the survivors felt about "Grandma's" entry into the eternal realm. "But she was so *good.*" What lays behind that comment is the statement, "We knew how she *really* was," and knowing her true nature and personality…

What doesn't fly then is the unbelievably good news that upon our deaths, Jesus is there to embrace us and to welcome us without referring to a checklist or preconditions. The words "*NOTHING* will separate us from the love of God in Christ Jesus" (Romans 8:30) get lost in the shuffle of guilt, insecurity, and unbelief (*belief* being *trust*). The good news, the gospel, is not heard, accepted, or trusted as a great comfort in the face of painful and terrible loss and a shaky faith that has been relegated to worship perhaps once in a great while, if that.

Many sermons, too, become more oriented toward what *we* are doing or are supposed to do. How many times have preachers challenged congregations to figure out what kind of soil they are, echoing the interpretation of the sower offered by the church? The church becomes a captive of morality lessons and, to use a Lutheran slogan, "the Law," instead of proclaiming with boldness the redeeming action of God in Christ, which we call "the gospel."

This is what happens to the Bible stories; when we forget that they are, in the last resort, about God and not about us, we easily lose sight of how the Bible is primarily God's story of redemption. Our personal experiences, our tragedies, our brokenness become the lens of viewing Scripture. The Bible can then become a handbook of morality lessons. Folks then wield the Bible as a go-to handbook of behavior. Perhaps starting at the very beginning of humanity's entry into the story will help us see this more clearly.

Where It All Began

The story of the Adam and Eve caper in the Garden of Eden need not be repeated here as the story is so well-known. (Adam and Eve are not named until later in the story, Eve in 3:20, Adam in 4:25; up to that point they are simply *man* and *woman*.) A brief comment about the serpent, however, is important because its appearance is a turning point in the blessedness of the Garden. Although many equate the serpent with the devil, or Satan (which is a later interpretation), there is no indication that the serpent is evil and has it in for the couple. Rather, the serpent acts like a literary device in that it creates the environment in which the innate human proclivity to do what it wants to do can come to the fore. After all, the serpent is part of the creation, which God found *very good*!

So we begin with Genesis 3:8–10:

> *They heard the sound of the LORD God walking in the garden at the time of the evening breeze, and the man and his wife hid themselves from the presence of the LORD God among the trees of the garden.*
>
> *But the LORD God called to the man, and said to him, "Where are you?"*
>
> *He said, "I heard the sound of you in the garden, and I was afraid, because I was naked; and I hid myself."*

It took me far too long to hear God's voice and question as anything else than that of a ticked-off old man—much as my own father's voice. I related very well to Adam's fear on a gut level. Later Christian theologians took these verses and helped create an understanding of "original sin." The logical consequences? The angry God who needs to be appeased. The God with the eternal Michelangelo frown on his brow. But why shouldn't we understand God's question not as the beginning of a rant leading to punishment but rather the first introduction of good news—the gospel?

For what else is the gospel except God taking the initiative, intentionally and deliberately seeking out fallen humanity, coming to, and walking among people who have fallen short of God's intent for them, and God offering an *invitation to reconciliation and restoration*? Why can't we hear words of *grace* in God's question—that unmerited, unearned love of God so freely given? Part of the problem we have with grace is that we are all, deep down, legalists at heart. St. Paul was referring to this when he wrote in Romans 2:14:

> *When Gentiles, who do not possess the law, do instinctively what the law requires, these, though not having the law, are a law to themselves. They show that* what the law requires is written on their hearts, *to which their own conscience also bears witness…* (my emphasis)

In other words, we approach life from a legalistic point of view that demands we fit into its structure—or we demand justice bend toward us. So we delight in that. And while that might be safe because we can supposedly control life more easily, it's ultimately not full of much grace, mercy, and forgiveness. There is, to be sure, far less worldly security in living as a new creature in Christ. After all, God's righteousness is incomprehensible to human beings outside of the gift of the Holy Spirit. Martin Luther, in his "*Small Catechism, The Apostles Creed,*" made the radical assertion that we believe that we cannot believe in Jesus outside of the gift of the Holy Spirit, who opens up for us the new life:

> *The Third Article: Sanctification*
> *What does this mean?*
> Answer: *I believe that by my own reason or strength, I cannot believe in Jesus Christ, my Lord, or come to him. But the Holy Spirit has called me through the gospel, enlightened me with his gifts, and sanctified and preserved me in true faith, just as he calls, gathers, enlightens, and sanctifies the whole Christian church on earth and preserves it in union with Jesus Christ in the one true faith.*

When Simon Peter responded to Jesus' question of, *"But who do you say that I am?"* he confessed Jesus as Messiah, the Son of the living God. And Jesus responded with *"Blessed are you, Simon son of Jonah! For flesh and blood has not revealed this to you, but my Father in heaven"* (Matthew 16:17).

So the Scriptures make clear and declare that even our faith is a gift from God, a gift of grace, because we—of our own accord, strength, or reasoning—cannot "make a decision for Jesus." After all, what is vital for faith is the truth that God in Christ Jesus has decided for us once and for all on the cross.

Yet in spite of the fact that we so often reject grace because it's not *fair,* according to how *we* function, God works this way. Perhaps that is why the "Parable of the Laborers in the Vineyard" is so *unfair*!

Life Ain't Easy

But what about the punishments that follow the disobedience of Adam and Eve? What God lays out in Genesis 3:14–19 is much more than a time-stamped slap on the wrist; they are exactly the same conditions under which we, too, labor in going about our daily living. But just how do these "punishments" jive with what Jesus says in the Sermon on the Mount:

> *But I say to you, "Love your enemies and pray for those who persecute you, so that you may be children of your Father in heaven; for makes his sun rise on the evil and on the good, and sends rain on the righteous and on the unrighteous."* (Matthew 5:44–45)

Now if Jesus came not to convince God to be more charitable toward his errant creatures but rather to open our eyes and hearts to the loving heart of God, how can one reconcile the punishments of Genesis 3 with Jesus' description of a God who loves unconditionally? A God who showers blessings upon *all* of God's creatures—deserving or not according to our sense of righteousness?

Maybe, just maybe, God did not send these punishments upon wayward humanity, but rather the writer of Genesis is portraying a God who is simply describing the *reality of daily life. "And [your husband] will rule over you"* (Genesis 3:16). There it is: the description of patriarchalism, subjection, second-class citizenship, the list goes on. The consequences? An imbalance in relationships, the "master of the house" syndrome, abuse, a stubborn rejection of the threatening absolute equality God intended for humanity, the scourge of those who want a fair shake.

Equality of the Sexes

Absolute equality? The Bible I use has 996 printed pages in the Hebrew Testament. The New Testament is 284 pages long. I know you can do the math, but that is a total of 1,280 pages. Genesis 1 and 2 (which is the story of God's intent) takes two pages until the risen Jesus says in the Revelation, 21:5, "*See, I am making all things new*"—1,278 pages of inequality, subjection, and all the *-isms* that divide us hold sway until the Lamb who was slain proclaims the end result of his victory: the cosmos restored in Genesis 1 and 2.

I hate buying cars. But whenever the two of us go to a dealership in search of a replacement vehicle, 95 percent of the time the salesperson comes right over to me, ignores my wife, even in the face of my telling the salesperson (the men do this far more than the women), "Please, talk to my wife." And that attitude is rampant even in the church. As a male pastor I have, to an extent, instant "credibility"; female pastors usually need to work harder to gain the credibility I usually effortlessly enjoy, whether that gift is deserved or not.

Whenever I mention this imbalance in layperson classes or during a Sunday sermon, I see the majority of heads nodding in agreement. Many of the experiences shared demonstrate this frustrating and sad reality, even in a society that proclaims, on paper, all people to be equal. Well, not yet.

Even in the extended Church there are many denominations that refuse to acknowledge that women, too, have gifts of the Spirit, one of which is the gift of prophecy—speaking God's Word to address a contemporary, real-life situation—better known as preaching.

Martin Luther of sixteenth century Reformation fame taught that men and women are equal in spiritual matters. *But* at home, the wife needs to be subordinate to the husband. Later, theologians excuse Luther by saying he was "a man of his times," and that explains (excuses!) his patriarchalism. George Washington was a slave owner, and he was also "a man of his times." But wrong is wrong, and while we might understand the reluctance of Luther to overturn society's norms too much and while we might understand the reluctance of Washington to ruin himself politically and financially by releasing his personal slaves during his lifetime, one cannot shrug one's shoulders. The message of the Bible is radical and is oftentimes toned down to make it more palatable, especially when it challenges the way things are done.

But what does the Bible say about this issue of equality? It starts out, as I mention over and over, in Genesis 1 and 2 with God's intent. The author of Genesis 1 (termed "the *Elohist*" because the writer uses the name "Elohim": [God]) states this:

> *So God created humankind in his image,*
> *in the image of God he created them;*
> *male and female he created them.* (Genesis 1:27)

I've maintained the poetic form of these verses because Hebrew uses *parallelism* in its poetry. Thus, one verse is helpful in interpreting another verse, indicating the same thought, image, or idea expressed differently. The Hebrew text uses the word *adam*, which is here translated as *humankind*. (This is not the individual Adam, who is named later, but the masculine gender noun *adam*.)

The next line *he created them* in Hebrew, which states he created *him*, referring back *grammatically* to *adam/humankind* of the previous verse. Then the brief poem states that Elohim created them male and female, both understood as being equal members of humankind. The creation of humanity story in Genesis 1 is pretty straightforward. Genesis 2 presents a whole other challenge: "*Then the* LORD *God formed man from the dust of the ground*" (Genesis 2:7).

Again, the word *adam* is used to identify this individual, who represents humanity. But an incomplete humanity because the story continues: "*Then the* LORD *God said, 'It is not good that the man should be alone; I will make him a helper as his partner."* In this second different yet same version of the creation of humanity, the LORD God (this writer is known as the Yahwist because the name for God is Yahweh, which, because of its extreme sacredness, is given the "code name" of LORD [hence the capital letter spelling]).

Nowadays the plumbers I contract with to service our home almost always bring along a partner—usually an individual who is learning the trade; the partner is the person who runs back to the truck for parts, hands the master plumber tools, and cleans up after the work is done. The partner is not equal to the certified plumber. So there is no equality there.

The Yahwist version of the creation story, however, is not calling the woman a "partner." The author is, in the original Hebrew, calling the woman "a power equal to" the man (an *ezer c'negdo*). So the equality of the sexes in Genesis 1 is maintained in Genesis 2, albeit by a totally different story line. Two different versions with the same result, making the same point. I will let the reader draw his or her own conclusions as to why translation committees…don't acknowledge this.

But we move on to Genesis 3 and the collapse of God's good creation. Need I mention how frustrating work can be? While I haven't been a butcher, baker, or candlestick maker, I have grunted my way through public school teaching, waitering, and parish work, in addition to what feels like dozens of temporary gigs throughout my life. Except when I was painting barns or reslating roofs during "vacation," I haven't earned my bread "by the sweat of my face," but I could write novels on the frustration that work causes, like anyone else could. This is reality.

So then verse 19 ends with this note: *"You shall eat bread until you return to the ground, for out of it you were taken; you are dust, and to dust you shall return."*

No One is Going to Live Forever

During the solemnity of the Ash Wednesday liturgy, we hear these same words as the ashes are applied to our foreheads: "*Remember that you are dust, and to dust you shall return.*"

I have been teaching in the Diakonia Program of the Grand Canyon Synod of the Evangelical Lutheran Church in America for several years now, guiding laypersons through five-week overviews of both Hebrew and Christian testaments. Without fail, when I ask the students how they understand these words, the answer is the same: God is punishing us with death, meaning physical death.

But what if God is, instead, saying something else to his wayward children: Remember that life is not eternal. What if I, God, am reminding you that, first of all, you are not God, and secondly, you are called to appreciate life for what it is—for it will end?

Of course, God had said earlier in Genesis 2:16ff: "*You may freely eat of every tree of the garden; but of the tree of the knowledge of good and evil you shall not eat, for in the day that you eat of it you shall die.*"

The serpent also drew upon this in talking to the woman: "*You will not die; for God knows that when you eat of it your eyes will be opened, and you will be like God, knowing good and evil*" (Genesis 3:4b–5).

But what death are we talking about here in these verses? Life is on a continuum, and the healthier one is, for example, the further away from death we are. Likewise, the greater the despair, illness, rejection, depression, and so on that affect us and tear down our humanity, as they can define us, the closer to death we are. Biological death is also an obvious answer.

Earlier in Genesis 2, God created a creature out of the dust of the earth, and God breathed into this clay ball the breath of life, and the man became a *nephesh*. In our English translations of the Bible, the word *nephesh* is often translated as *soul*—"*He restores my soul*" (Psalm 23:3a), for example.

But notice that the newer translations of Psalm 23 render "*I shall dwell in the house of the* LORD *forever*" as "*my whole life long*"— the translation change acknowledges not a believer's endless, eternal dwelling in the house of the LORD but rather the blessing of dwelling in the temple as long as life lasts. What the word *nephesh* seems to indicate is that we are born, we live, and we die. It is a natural, biological process, which the ancient peoples of the Bible oftentimes accepted far more graciously than we in our death-defying culture. In our society, people "pass" or "go to their eternal rest." The word *die* is studiously avoided. While early Hebrew Scriptures describe the dead as "shades," forgotten by God (see Psalm 88), there is no description of heaven as Christians have come to believe in, and Hebrew thought only gradually and very slowly developed a concept of an afterlife, surely strongly influenced by the Babylonian Exile, where the Exiles, now known as Jews, came into contact with other religions that had a more developed concept of the afterlife.

Of course, this understanding is *pre-Easter*, for it is the resurrection of Jesus from the dead that has made all the difference in the lives of Christian believers. But it's a hard sell as we are conditioned by popular culture, unduly influenced by ancient Greek philosophical dualism to think that we zoom automatically into the heavenly realm. To think that we might actually, literally, *die* is, to be sure, frightening. But how then is resurrection good news if we don't die? After all, Jesus himself experienced the terrors of death, but it was his faithfulness, his trust in God, that caused God to raise him on the third day.

By the time of chapter 6 in Genesis, we get the sense of God's total frustration with an evermore sinning humanity to the point that God says, "*I am sorry that I have made people.*" The final decision? To "*make an end of all flesh, for the earth is filled with violence because of (people); now I am going to destroy them along with the earth*" (Genesis 6:13).

THE GREAT FLOOD

As a child, I used to leaf through my father's Sunday School book, a woodcut of the great flood drawing my attention time and again, perhaps because of its scary, gloomy imagery and unspoken message. Against a dark and rainy background floated an ark, while in the foreground, several people plus various animals were clinging to a tiny mountain peak, apparently trying in their terror and hopelessness to get the attention of those safely ensconced in the ark as the waters relentlessly mounted.

We often forget that the Hebrew peoples told stories to get across their theological point; and arguing whether there was a great flood or not, whether the real ark has been found, and dwelling on the destruction of the world, takes the focus off what Martin Luther in his *Flood Prayer* stresses: "*By the waters of the flood you condemned the wicked and saved those whom you had chosen, Noah and his family. You led Israel by a pillar of cloud and fire through the sea, out of slavery into the freedom of the promised land*" (*Lutheran Book of Worship*, pg.122).

That is, the great flood, while a mightily dramatic tale, is, in the last resort, less about the destruction of the world (which is just, according to our sense of justice) and more about how God saves God's people in times of chaos, misery, trouble, and destruction. (I fully recognize how trite and questionable this sounds, writing only a few decades after the Holocaust while Holocaust survivors are still alive. I wonder how theologians will address that horrid era a hundred or two hundred years from now, when all the witnesses are long gone, and the gradual perspective of time allows a less emotional gut reaction to Nazi genocide.)

But what about God reaching the limit of mercy in the flood story? Is it possible that we transfer to God our own sense and understanding of justice, our own sense of righteousness, our own sense of indignation, forgetting that God is a God of infinite compassion?

Psalm 137 is a *historical/imprecatory* (accusatory) psalm, describing the utter frustration of the exiles languishing in Babylon during the sixth century BC. The opening verses are lyrical and beautiful poetry:

> *By the rivers of Babylon—there we sat down and there we wept when we remembered Zion. On the willows there we hung up our harps. For there our captors asked us for songs, and our tormentors asked for mirth, saying, "Sing us one of the songs of Zion!"* (Psalm 137:1–3)

But how many worship services include the last two verses as part of the appointed psalmody: *"O daughter Babylon, you devastator! Happy shall they be who pay you back what you have done to us! Happy shall they be who take your little ones and dash them against the rock"* (Psalm 137:8–9)!

Yikes. If we live strictly according to the Bible…

It is clear that this psalm contains a lot—a whole lot—of human frustration. Several generations of Jews had been forcibly held against their will, suffering the mockery of their conquerors, whose pagan gods had vanquished and driven Yahweh into the ground, or so they thought. Knowing that necessary historical context, the *Sitz im Leben*, we need to separate the understandably human emotions from God, who, again, *"makes his sun rise on the evil and on the good."* And perhaps, we need to sift out the human judgment from a God who loves the world—even if, according to the Bible, God expresses exasperation at times.

The Conquest and Extermination

Perhaps one of the most problematic sections of the Hebrew Bible deals with the conquest as the former Hebrew slaves enter Canaan to claim their inheritance. Chapter after chapter details brutal and agonizing murder of all forms of life in the vanquished cities of the Canaanites. The story of Joshua and the Battle of Jericho is perhaps the best known of these stories:

> *As soon as the people heard the sound of the trumpets, they raised a great shout, and the wall fell down flat; so the people charged straight ahead into the city and captured it. Then they devoted to destruction by the edge of the sword all in the city, both men and women, young and old, oxen, sheep, and donkeys.* (Joshua 6:20)

This pattern of destruction is repeated often in Joshua, with the Canaanite population suffering what is presented as a brutal, divinely inspired, thorough ethnic cleansing. Those who have turned against God in modern times often refer to these incidents as a reason for not worshiping—a butcher God. How can a *loving* God demand the total destruction of a people who are just going about their daily lives?

There is really no way to justify this unfortunate pattern of ethnic cleansing. So what do we make of it? The stories are in the Bible, and we need to consider them seriously and deal with them, even if they are, for the most part, ignored in corporate worship.

In the book following Joshua, Judges, the local populations curiously *still* seem to be thriving and a nuisance and are creating an ongoing problem for the newcomers in the Promised Land. Hence the rise of Judges, who strove to keep the Israelites living in safety. Can the total wipeout of the local populations in Joshua be reconciled with the need for Israel to have temporary military leaders to save them from these very same people, as in Judges?

So maybe, just maybe, the "idealistic" portrayal of the conquest in Joshua was not quite the reality of attempting to root out the indigenous peoples. Maybe, just maybe, this book is a "wish it happened this way" story, balanced by the seemingly more realistic history of Judges. But why?

The Call of God's People

What often gets lost in the dramatic shuffle of wars, sieges, battles, and such is the overarching purpose for God's people to exist. Going back to Genesis 12, where God calls Abram/Abraham (and Sarai/Sarah) to be the bearer(s) of blessing to the world:

> *I will make of you a great nation, and I will bless you and make your name great, so that you will be a blessing. I will bless those who bless you, and the one who curses you I will curse; and in you all the families of the earth shall be blessed.* (Genesis 12:2–3)

The call to be a chosen people runs through the entire Hebrew Scriptures, even if that divine call gets sidetracked by war, idolatry, syncretism, social injustice, and the like. *Chosenness* is passive grammatically; it means that one has been chosen by someone else (God, in this case). It further does not mean that one is chosen for any personal virtuous attributes or due to the worthiness of the elect but rather that one has been chosen for a purpose: to demonstrate to the world that God is a god who wants to be recognized for blessing all people. Then in return, people would worship/respect/honor God for who God is. This is what St. Paul is writing about in Romans 1:21: "*For though they (who suppress the truth—about God) knew God, they did not honor him as God or give thanks to him, but they became futile in their thinking, and their senseless minds were darkened.*"

Abraham several times receives reassurance from God that it is his, Abraham's, trust that is commended as faith. We applaud that. After hearing these words of gracious promise in chapter 12, he immediately travels in faith into the unknown promised land. Then faced with famine, he wends his way to Egypt. Abraham then tries to take things into his own hands when he perceived a threat to *his* life by the Egyptians. So he instructs Sarah to tell the Egyptian officials that she is Abraham's sister to preserve his own life. But then "*The Lord afflicted Pharoah and his house with great plagues because of Sarai, Abram's wife*" (Genesis 12:17).

There's a lesson here for all of us: When the person of faith does not act in accordance with the trust she or he placed in God, others are not blessed but often can and do suffer. (A similar story is recorded in Genesis 20, where God warns King Abimelech that he is about to die because of Sarai and her married status.)

At the end of Genesis, this life of being a blessing to others is also important in the Joseph story, for he becomes a blessing to Potiphar and eventually the entire land of Egypt, thus fulfilling his calling and being an example for us. As a result of his steadfastness of faith, his own clan's people are saved from famine as he declares to his brothers in Genesis 50:19–20:

> *Do not be afraid! Am I in the place of God?*
> *Even though you intended to do harm to me, God*
> *intended it for good, in order to preserve a numerous*
> *people, as he is doing today.*

Perhaps this understanding of carrying the blessings of God would be a better impetus for evangelism. Rather than drag people kicking and screaming into congregations "to fill the pews," we ought better witness to how God has blessed us so that others may recognize the goodness of God in their own lives and thereby honor, thank, and worship God.

This isn't a matter of digressing from the issues raised above as to how a loving God can demand blood sacrifice. Rather, the human impulse to create a narrative that is more favorable, that is, comfortable, to the tellers than the possibilities of what really happened results in Joshua in the Hebrews steamrolling the local populace without pity. Perhaps there is a hint of God's priority when Joshua meets the commander of the army of the LORD prior to the fall of Jericho; in response to Joshua's query, *"Are you for us or against us?"* the armed man responds, *"Neither"* (Joshua 5:13–14).

Maybe this strange response isn't so strange at all, coming from God's representative. For God is for us, and not against us, and is intent on keeping the promise given to Abraham alive through the Israelites at this point in time, later through Hebrews and Jews, and ultimately also granted to the Gentile followers of Jesus.

Being a Blessing Sometimes Comes Last

There is, of course, a huge amount of material that is the result of the failure of God's chosen people to be faithful in their stewardship of blessing. Time and again, many kings proved to be poor instruments of God's intents, the prophets railed against syncretism, injustice, and perhaps the worst of all, a downright blasé attitude toward Yahweh: "*He will not do good or evil*" (Zephaniah 1:12).

Sounds an awful like today's contemptuous attitudes toward God and the faith! But Yahweh was preparing to judge those "*who rest complacently on their dregs*" (Zephaniah 1:12).

Often the prophets spoke of unimaginable suffering due to exile, diaspora, and invasion, even while God again and again promised a brighter future, lived under the lordship of Yahweh. This is the God who proclaimed in Hosea:

> *How can I give you up, Ephraim? How can I hand you over, O Israel? How can I make you like Admah? How can I treat you like Zeboiim? My heart recoils within me; my compassion grows warm and tender. I will not execute my fierce anger; I will not again destroy Ephraim; for I am God and no mortal, the Holy One in your midst, and I will not come in wrath.* (Hosea 11:8–11)

But aren't we more like Jonah, who complained that his preaching was successful and that the inhabitants of Ninevah repented—thus causing God to say:

> *And should I not be concerned about Ninevah, that great city in which there are more than a hundred and twenty thousand persons who do not know their right hand from their left, and also many animals? (Jonah 4:11)*

Grace extended to the undeserving (which includes all of us, by the way) strangely elicits an uncharitable, harsh response. Because grace isn't "fair"; it goes against deeply ingrained human notions of right and wrong. Yet this is how God operates.

And the foremost example of grace in action is none other than Jesus of Nazareth to whom we now turn.

PART 2

THE GOSPEL ACCORDING TO JESUS

Jesus the Teacher of Good News

On more than one occasion, Jesus is called Teacher in the gospel accounts. His favorite teaching medium was the parable:

> *Jesus told the crowds all these things in parables; without a parable he told them nothing. This was to fulfill what had been spoken through the prophet: "I will open my mouth to speak in parables; I will proclaim what has been hidden from the foundation of the world." (Matthew 13:35)*

As we read in Mark 1:14, the content of his teaching is the gospel (of God), the good news of God's kingdom: "*Now after John was arrested, Jesus came to Galilee, proclaiming the good news of God, and saying, 'The time is fulfilled, and the kingdom of God has come near; repent, and believe in the good news.*'"

Now the term "Kingdom of God" is another way of expressing "the ruling activity of God in the world." That is, the Kingdom of God is not some distant nebulous heavenly abode in the stratosphere, whose existence we can only long for and must wait to experience only postmortem. Rather, God's activity in the daily give-and-take of human relationships is the leaven, the salt, the light, that makes kingdom living a possibility in the here and now. Have you ever, for example, been forgiven, or have you ever forgiven someone else? If you answer *yes*, you have experienced the Kingdom of God in this life. That is, the Kingdom is "*already, not yet,*" as is said among theologians.

But so often the teachings of Jesus have become a new law, a yoke, according to Acts 15:10, where Peter in the midst of a rather hot and heavy debate about requiring circumcision for newly converted Gentiles, says this to the apostles and elders:

> *Now, therefore, why are you putting God to the test by placing on the neck of the disciples a yoke (the Law) that neither our ancestors nor we have been able to bear? On the contrary, we believe that we will be saved through the grace of the Lord Jesus, just as they (the Gentiles) will. (Acts 15:10–11)*

PARABLES ARE ABOUT *GOD*

What often happens is that the original meaning of the parable, Jesus' intent on telling it so as to proclaim good news, is clouded by the interpretations offered by the gospel writers, attempts to help the young developing Church in its struggle not only to define itself to its new membership but also as a tool of evangelism. Just as John's gospel account uses *signs* (*not* miracles) (such as turning water into wine, healing the blind man, raising Lazarus), both to create and strengthen and sustain faith among believers, so too can the parables be used to guide and strengthen the faith of God's people.

So let's take a look at the parable of the Good Samaritan. This beloved story is so well-known that even the term "Good Samaritan" is used freely by the nonreligious to describe one who, with good intentions, performs a good deed to someone in crisis. Here is the parable set within the context of a question about eternal life and what one must do to obtain it:

> Just then a lawyer stood up to test Jesus. "Teacher," he said, "what must I do to inherit eternal life?"
>
> He said to him, "What is written in the law? What do you read there?"
>
> He answered, "You shall love the Lord your God with all your heart, and will all your soul, and with all your strength, and with all your mind; and your neighbor as yourself."
>
> And he said to him, "You have given the right answer; do this, and you will live."

But wanting to justify himself, he asked Jesus, "And who is my neighbor?"

Jesus replied: *"A man was going down from Jerusalem to Jericho, and fell into the hands of robbers, who stripped him, beat him, and went away, leaving him half dead. Now by chance a priest was going down that road; and when he saw him, he passed by on the other side. So likewise a Levite, when he came to the place and saw him, passed by on the other side. But a Samaritan while travelling came near him; and when he saw him, he was moved with pity. He went to him and bandaged his wounds, having poured oil and wine on them. Then he put him on his own animal, brought him to an inn, and took care of him. The next day he took out two denarii, gave them to the innkeeper, and said, 'Take care of him; and when I come back, I will repay you whatever more you spend.'* Which of these three do you think was a neighbor to the man who fell into the hands of the robbers?"

He said, "The one who showed mercy."

Jesus said to him, "Go and do likewise." (Luke 10:25–37)

The *text set in roman* represents the *context* in which the gospel writer placed this most wonderful parable. The *italicized text* represents the parable itself. The parable answers the question for the lawyer, i.e., possibly the developing church, as to who exactly should be a neighbor and recipient of the church's ministry. "*The one who showed mercy.*" And the ethical exhortation follows immediately: "*Go and do likewise.*"

Going and doing likewise is right up our alley because not only does Jesus command that we help the neighbor in need, but also then we are in control of the situation. Wait. What?

This is the uncomfortable truth touched upon in this story: Just how easy it is for any single one of us to ask for help? Our stubbornness, our pride, our delusion that we are in control of life and every-thing that happens to us stand in the way of saying, "I need help," for a whole lot of people. Asking for help is seen as a sign of weakness. Not being "in charge" of a situation raises questions for ourselves and others, that we are not totally competent. It's the old sinfulness of Adam and Eve raising its head again. We will do what *we* want to do because we are in control/charge. Well, not.

It is legitimate that Luke adds this context involving the lawyer even if I am suggesting that the historical Jesus did not necessarily say these words because, and *this is important*, Jesus speaks *then as now* through the Church. So isolating the parable from the *Sitz im Leben*, as it were, leaves us with just the original parable (which runs from verses 30 to 35), which again is the italicized text.

We will remember that Jesus' teaching and preaching concerned the good news of God—meaning that *this* is what we are to look for in the parables. So there are two cautions that are helpful in recovering the intent of Jesus to proclaim the good news of God in his storytelling:

The parables in original form are not allegories. Simply put, the characters in the parables should not be equated with this or that person.

And *do not understand the parables as morality lessons.*

"The Parable of the Widow and the Unjust Judge" is one such example (Luke 18:1–8) as is "The Parable of the Unjust Steward" (Luke 16:1–9). If Jesus were to say in the parables that these are lessons in morality and ethical behavior, "*And I tell you, make friends for yourselves by means of dishonest wealth so that when it is gone, they may welcome you into the eternal homes,*" we must then conclude that he is commending dishonesty.

The third point is what allows us to recapture the good news in the parables: *Do look for God's activity in the parables.* There is a caution: we need to be consistent in interpreting the parables. That means we just can't change the guidelines in concluding more comfortable for us and therefore less challenging as we struggle with God's Word.

So let us reconsider "The Parable of the Good Samaritan" and apply these simple guidelines to what Jesus says. As mentioned previously, the parable itself is isolated from Luke's context in which the lawyer asks, "*Who is my neighbor?*"

Now much is often made about the manner in which the Levite and the priest, professional religious persons, conducted themselves in avoiding the victim. While one might excuse their avoidance in that they were just following the Levitical rules for ritual purity, they are not absolutely essential to the story's essence, except perhaps to demonstrate "anti"-neighborliness. So the prime mover in the parable is a questionable character. His presence front and center in the story would be disturbing to listeners. Historically, Samaritans were outcasts in Jewish society, and a righteous Jew would not allow him- or herself be in their company. But it is this one, a representative of this despised group of people, who rescues and thereby saves the life of the robbery victim. What is *God* doing in this parable, keeping in mind that the parable is first and foremost about what *God is* doing? Or perhaps better expressed, what is the action that expresses the Kingdom of God, God's ruling activity, among us?

The heart of the story is that a person who is near death who cannot in any way, shape, or form help him- or herself out of dire circumstances is given life by another. Now while we think we have life under our control, one of our greatest illusions, the reality of things is that we simply cannot redeem ourselves, be that redemption in life or redemption from death. It takes a source of help outside of us to do this. This is God's activity. But what also makes this parable so radical is that it equates God with a despised one.

God coming to us in the person of an addict—who reaches out to us? The homeless? The alien? That is, if we were totally honest and had our druthers, we would reject God's advances on our part. Our human nature (apart from the gift of the Holy Spirit) cannot abide God reaching out to us; it is an admission that we are not in control, that we are ultimately powerless, and that God does for us what we cannot possibly do for ourselves.

Paul in Romans 5:8ff expresses this deep, troubling truth, albeit using different words:

> *But God proves his love for us in that while we were still sinners Christ died for us... For if while we were enemies, we were reconciled to God through the death of his Son, much more surely, having been reconciled, will we be saved by his life.*

I've let Paul express the dark truth about humanity's relationship vis-à-vis God: we are *enemies* of the Holy One apart from knowing God through Jesus Christ, and we reject God's love because we are powerless to accept this mysterious love that pursues us relentlessly. For *we* are the one lying helpless in the ditch, nearing death, and yet God comes to us, rescuing us from the power of sin, death, and the devil. In other words, this parable is a parable about *justification by grace*. God's love is demonstrated even before we can respond to God's saying "yes!" to us.

Some denominations make much ado about the ancient practice of infant baptism, which is practiced in my Church. One of their objections is correct—one looks in vain in the New Testament to cite an occasion when an infant was baptized. The closest one can get in attempting to proof text this rite is that households were baptized, but the household might include the cow, the donkey, and the goats living under the same roof. Rather, infant baptism is the powerful symbol of God's grace coming to us when we are the most helpless we will ever be. It's called *prevenient grace*, a theological description of the meaning of the ancient rite.

But what about the Lukan context, "*Who is my neighbor?*" Because we are first justified, we can go out and serve our neighbor in need, not because we will be saved by our works (we are saved prior to doing works) but because we can now act in freedom from trying to impress God. Set free by grace, we can respond out of gratitude and thanksgiving to the one who has, in the first place, redeemed us.

As Luther emphasized, God doesn't need our good works but our neighbor does. So both the isolated, original parable and the Lukan context are valuable and instructive for the followers of Jesus.

Knowing that God in Jesus has redeemed us and therefore saved us, our good works can be accomplished more freely without worrying if we have done enough or not to please or influence God toward us. That decision has already been made.

One of Luther's greatest writings is entitled *The Freedom of a Christian* (1520), in which he explores early in the Reformation this astounding truth:

"In this tract, Luther eloquently explores the paradox of Christian freedom: a believer in both an *utterly free lord of all, subject to none,* and *an utterly dutiful servant to all, subject to everyone.* By faith alone, God sets a person completely free in Christ, yet love binds them to serve their neighbor" (www.enotes.com/topics/freedom-Christian).

For Luther, it is a matter of acting out of agape love (serving love) in response to the agape love on the cross (John 3:16) that saved us.

Luke 15 is known as the "Lost and Found" chapter of this gospel account because there are three lost/found/rejoicing parables. The longer one is entitled "The Prodigal Son" and is paired with the parables of the lost coin and the lost sheep. The context? The usual grousing and complaining of religious authorities:

> *Now all the tax collectors and sinners were com-*
> *ing near to listen to him. And the Pharisees and the*
> *scribes were grumbling and saying, "This fellow wel-*
> *comes sinners and eats with them." (Luke 15:1–2)*

The two introductory parables are brief and express the same divine truth that God relentlessly seeks the lost and that when the lost is found (notice the coin cannot find itself, neither can the wayward sheep), there is great rejoicing in heaven—meaning that God is mightily pleased.

"The Prodigal Son" fleshes out this defining characteristic of God that God seeks the lost. From a strictly legal Mosaic point of view, the younger son has condemned himself with his profligate actions:

> *If someone has a stubborn and rebellious son*
> *who will not obey his father and mother, who does*

> *not heed them when they discipline him, then his father and his mother shall take hold of him and bring him out to the elders of his town at the gate of that place. They shall say to the elders of his town, "This son of ours is stubborn and rebellious. He will not obey us. He is a glutton and a drunkard." Then all the men of the town shall stone him to death. So you shall purge the evil from your midst; and all Israel will hear, and be afraid.* (Deuteronomy 21:18ff)

It's not clear that this punishment was ever carried out in ancient Israel, but the Deuteronomy passage demonstrates the contrast between what was expected of fathers and mothers regarding their rebellious children and Jesus' take on such people. The Law of Moses was pretty straightforward in how to respond to a prodigal son. Jesus upends this. As he says in the passage about divorce, one might have the legal standing to do the deed, but it is done out of hardness of heart. He offers the better way.

Wondrous words of grace are spoken after the return of the prodigal son: *"For this son of mine was dead and is alive again; he was lost and is found"* (Luke 15:32), and the party began.

Yet the dynamics leading to this reconciliation, resulting in full restoration of sonship, are worth looking at more closely. What happened between *"He would gladly have filled himself with the pods that the pigs were eating; and no one gave him anything"* (Luke 15:16) and the father's embrace and kiss?

The turn comes in the son's evaluation of his personal miserable circumstance:

> *But when he came to himself, he said, "How many of my father's hired hands have bread enough and to spare, but here I am dying of hunger! I will get up and go to my father, and I will say to him, 'Father, I have sinned against heaven and before you;*

*I am no longer worthy to be called your son; treat
me like one of our hired hands."* (Luke 15:17–19)

The son practices his rehearsed speech because his very life, his existence, his βίος, depends on his father accepting him again. But note what happens: even *before* the son can repeat his speech of repentance, the father is filled with compassion. When the son is far off, he gets up and runs (which is undignified for a patriarchal type), embraces, and kisses the wayward child. Only then does the son give his speech. What follows the speech is this critical word *but*. *But* negates all that comes before. How wonderful to have someone say to you, "*I love you.* But *you should lose fifteen pounds.*" What follows *but* destroys what comes before! So for Luke, the practiced speech, which might be truly heartfelt or simply self-serving out of desperation, is not necessary for the son to be fully restored. The father's pleasure is to do that regardless of motive; only turn to God and live, it is saying, regardless of one's motive. That's radical and might not sit well with some folks.

Again, this is a parable of justification by grace. It doesn't matter to the father if the son is truly repentant or truly manipulative; what matters is that the son has returned, the lost has been found. "*But we had to celebrate*" is said to disapproving older son. While the older son might or might not represent Judaism, the sad fact is that grace extended to the unworthy is more often rejected by the uptight upright than not. So it might be worthwhile to rename this parable, which is ultimately not about a prodigal son but a *prodigal* father. *Prodigal* is one of those words that has multiple meanings; we know the first common meaning well because of the son's unconscionable lifestyle: *wasteful, spendthrift, imprudent,* and so on. The secondary meaning? *Generous, unstinting unsparing*—this describes the father who gives love and offers acceptance on a lavish, generous basis yet is often treated with contempt by others. Yet rather than rename the parable "*The Prodigal Father*" (because it could possibly unintentionally send the wrong message), perhaps "*The Parable of the Compassionate Father*" would hit the mark. The attitude of the older obedient son is so characteristic for those who are more than happy to justify themselves.

> *Listen! For all these years, I have been working like a slave for you, and I have never disobeyed your command; yet you have never given me even a young goat so that I might celebrate with my friends. But when this son of yours came back, who has devoured your property with prostitutes, you killed the fatted calf for him!* (Luke 15:29–30)

And reject grace.

GRACE

But grace is not meant to be an excuse for continued behavior that strays, not from the "straight and narrow" but rather from God's invitation to live a new life dedicated to the service of the neighbor. The martyred German pastor and theologian Dietrich Bonhoeffer, who died at the hands of the Nazis in a concentration camp just days before its liberation by the Allies, called that understanding of grace "cheap."

> *Cheap grace is the grace we bestow on ourselves. Cheap grace is the preaching for forgiveness without requiring repentance, baptism without church discipline, Communion without confession... Cheap grace is grace without discipleship, grace without the cross, grace without Jesus Christ, living and incarnate.* (Dietrich Bonhoeffer, www.goodreads.com/quotes/83530-cheap-grace-is-the-grace-we-bestow-on-ourselves)

We know that the grace offered by God comes at a cost to God: the cross. But the issue of how to deal with those who faltered either in their commitment to God in Jesus or who wanted to take advantage of the offered gift oftentimes has consumed believers.

During the second century AD there was a persecution under the Roman emperor, Decius, sometime between AD 149 and 153. Christians were, as usual, refusing to honor the emperor as lord; the empire gave certificates to those who did, and this civic duty, even if perfunctory, created a conflict with the followers of Jesus.

"Jesus is Lord" is an early creed mentioned in Paul's writings (Romans 10:9, for example), and believers would be unable to say, even if just mouthing the words to get this civic duty over with, *"Caesar is lord."* When many believers folded under the political pressure, the situation created a crisis with early, still-developing Christianity. This crisis became known as the Rigorist/Laxist controversy. The Church was divided as to how to reintegrate former or weaker members who had caved in to the state's pressure but desired to return to the fold after the political demand had faded away. Rigorists were, as the name suggests, those who felt returnees needed to undergo a lengthy penance to redeem themselves before being accepted into the flock again. Laxists, as the name suggests, felt grace and mercy should be the compassionate means of welcoming the backsliders. A more gracious reconciliation, it was felt, was the more Christlike pathway. Grace did abound but not without yet another disagreement in the Church. If anything, the controversy again points out the reluctance of many to trust the good news: God graciously and mercifully accepts the lost who turn/return to God.

Immediately following the "Lost and Found" chapter of Luke is a troubling parable known as *"The Dishonest Steward/Manager."* Now if one were to make this a morality lesson, how would one justify this behavior? The master *"commended the dishonest manager because he had acted shrewdly; for the children of this age are more shrewd in dealing with their own generation than are the children of light. And I tell you, make friends for yourselves by means of dishonest wealth so that when it is gone, they may welcome you into the eternal homes"* (Luke 16:8–9).

Isolating the original parable (Luke 16:1–8a) from the end comments again still leaves us with a troubling story; the manager, while trying to secure his own future, is still not being honest about the debts owed the master. Through his actions, he ingratiates himself with the debtors, who will presumably (hopefully!) welcome him into their homes when he is dismissed from his present position. Luke's confusing comments following the parable itself don't help one to understand quickly what the issue is.

It doesn't sound like there is much to go on if this parable is about how God acts or the ruling activity of God in the world, which is the hallmark of the kingdom. Again, Luke's conclusion must be read carefully multiple times to find good news there.

First of all, trying to force good news out of dishonesty is a tough assignment admittedly. However, one must keep in mind that the parable *does* contain elements of justification. The manager is not acting differently than the prodigal son, in that he recognizes where his future lies, and he takes steps to secure it. Again, boldly, one might say. From *our* perspective, the manager is manipulative, and yet from *God's* perspective the end result is what truly matters—turning to God, even if one's motives aren't the purest. Even if our motivation is self-preservation, God rejoices if we turn to God. The father who embraced his wayward son even before hearing the rehearsed confession is the same god who simply wants us to turn to God. This is difficult to wrap one's mind around because we are called to be "pure in heart," and yet what individual has motives that are 100 percent pure in anything?

So we turn to yet another parable, that of "*The Widow and the Unjust Judge*" (Luke 18:1–8). The parable itself runs from verses 2 to 5, and the Lukan context is encouragement of unceasing prayer, a noble goal for a believer regardless of the circumstances described.

The figure of the judge is alarming; he has no regard for either God or human. He is continually approached by a widow who relentlessly asks for justice. So just to get rid of her, he grants her request, which he calls "justice." What is striking is that one does not really know if her request is just or not. She frankly just harps and harps until he can't take it any longer. So without considering the justice or injustice of her demands, he finds in her favor.

The Lukan conclusion of the parable (verse 5) is once more somewhat confusing, and one is again cautioned not to make this story a morality lesson. So, preachers, beware; it shows up in Year C, Proper 24, Pentecost XIX. But it's here in the New Testament. Is there good news to be found in the story of a harping widow and an unjust official?

Once again, we are called to look at this parable through the lens of justification by grace. The unjust judge *justifies* the persistent widow, not based upon the righteousness of her cause (which we don't know) but rather because of her constant badgering. Set within the context of consistent, persistent, and relentless prayer, God's grace justifies the sinner regardless of how righteous or unrighteous the cause. This is how our God acts. It's a stunning exposé of God, accepting the one who turns to God regardless of how "religious" that person is, or even their motivation. And if anything, God knows what really lies in the heart of the individual, and the parables demonstrate God's unconditional grace.

The Year of the Lord's Favor. The Day

The idea of grace is not, however, limited solely to the parables. St. Luke reports that after the temptation, Jesus returned to Galilee. When he came to Nazareth, he returned to his local synagogue, was handed the Isaiah scroll, and quoted from Isaiah 61:

> *The Spirit of the Lord is upon me, because he has anointed me to bring good news to the poor. He has sent me to proclaim release to the captives and recovery of sight to the blind, to let the oppressed go free, to proclaim the year of the Lord's favor.* (Luke 4:18–19)

The Isaiah context is the end of the Babylonian Exile of the sixth century BC with its promise of restoration, the vindication of God's people, and the new creation, among other blessings. Perhaps what Jesus does *not* say is a hint of what type of ministry he is going to undertake. The full verse 2 of Isaiah 61 is this: "*To proclaim the year of the Lord's favor, the day of vengeance of our God; to comfort all who mourn...*"

"*The day of vengeance of our God...*" Israel had, over the centuries since the Exodus, trusted that God would intervene to rectify the injustices, dangers, chaos, and challenges that threatened the chosen people. When their backs were against the Red Sea, the weakened tribes of the former Hebrew slaves were confronted with death by drowning or death by pharaoh's forces. Moses cried out to the people in Exodus 14:13–14:

> *Do not be afraid, stand firm, and see the deliverance that the LORD will accomplish for you today; for the Egyptians whom you see today you shall never see again. The LORD will fight for you, and you have only to keep still.*

The tribal God of the Hebrew slaves morphed into a heavenly, divine warrior who would intervene at moments of great crisis to deliver the people. When God is called the "Lord of Hosts" (Lord God of Sabaoth in older liturgical language), it calls upon this image of the warrior God. Another intervention mentioned in 2 Kings 19:32ff–37 describes the complete rout of the terrifying Assyrian, King Sennacherib:

> *Therefore thus says the LORD concerning the king of Assyria: He shall not come into this city, shoot an arrow there, come before it with a shield, or cast up a siege-ramp against it. By the way that he came, by the same he shall return; he shall not come into this city, says the LORD. For I will defend this city to save it, for my own sake and for the sake of my servant David. That very night the angel of the LORD set out and struck down one hundred eighty-five thousand in the camp of the Assyrians; when morning dawned, they were all dead bodies. Then King Sennacherib of Assyria left, went home, and lived at Nineveh.*

We see in these incidents the concept of the Day of the Lord coming together: a day on which Yahweh would enter time and space, destroy (again and finally) the enemies of Israel in order to restore the fortunes of the chosen people. It would truly be a *day of vengeance of our God.* Yet by the time of some of the prophets, the warning was that the chosen people themselves would now be the subject of

Yahweh's wrath because of their failure to observe the covenants God had made with their ancestors. These failures were very specific and particular, not just a general concept of "sinfulness."

> *Thus says the LORD: For three transgressions of Israel, and for four, I will not revoke the punishment; because they sell the righteous for silver, and the needy for a pair of sandals—they who trample the head of the poor into the dust of the earth, and push the afflicted out of the way: father and son go into the same girl, so that my holy name is profaned; they lay themselves down beside every altar on garments taken in pledge; and in the house of their God they drink wine bought with fines they imposed.* (Amos 2:6–8)

Amos warns the people that they are mistaken if they think they are immune from the consequences of their infidelity to Yahweh:

> *On that day, says the Lord GOD, I will make the sun go down at noon, and darken the earth in broad daylight. I will turn your feasts into mourning, and all your songs into lamentation; I will bring sackcloth on all loins, and baldness on every head; I will make it like the mourning for an only son, and the end of it like a bitter day.* (Amos 8:9–10)

Surely, God had copious reasons to punish Israel for their faithlessness, and yet the people persisted in thinking they would not be the subject of God's wrath against injustice. Chosenness morphed into the illusion that they could ignore God as he dictates:

> *Alas for you who desire the day of the LORD! Why do you want the day of the LORD? It is darkness, not light; as if someone fled from a lion, and was met by a bear; or went into the house and rested a hand against the wall, and was bitten by a snake.*

> *Is not the day of the LORD darkness, not light, and*
> *gloom with no brightness in it?* (Amos 5:18–20)

The warning is clear: "*Indeed, I am raising up against you a nation, O house of Israel, says the LORD, the God of hosts, and they shall oppress you from Leo-hamath to the Wadi Arabah*" (Amos 6:14).

In the course of history, the northern kingdom of Israel was invaded by the Assyrians in 722 BC; the people were scattered far and wide, and the nation ceased to exist as an independent entity. Once again, we come to the proposition that God is the one behind the destruction of Israel.

Do we need to defend God's reputation as the Righteous One who allows misery to descend upon the people of Israel? Or are *Israel's* attempts to disregard God's intent for a just society that paves the way for the rampant corruption so widely condemned by the prophets and, therefore, the deadly conclusions that engulfed both kingdoms because they had lost their focus? Indeed, the prophets speak to these issues without mincing their words. And yet is it possible to understand the historical events not as Yahweh's direct action but rather Yahweh allowing the people to experience the consequences of their unfaithful lives?

The individual I mentioned in the introduction pushed me to examine my own thoughts and theology about how exactly God deals with a rampantly out-of-control humanity, which God loves dearly in spite of how we all act.

Perhaps Martin Luther's image of the two hands of God is helpful. While Luther himself did not formally and directly state this concept, it is drawn from his interpretation of Scripture and other writings. But it is a convenient way to consider exactly how God interacts with the world, so I use the image. Luther said that the *left hand* of God demonstrates and represents how God works indirectly through secular authorities and the normal day-to-day events that make up our lives. The metaphor of God's *right hand* demonstrates and represents how God works in matters of grace, mercy, and salvation. And the right hand is "heavier" than the left—because God is a God of grace, mercy, and compassion. Ed Schroeder, in his précis of Philip Jenkins' book, *The Next Christendom* (Oxford University Press, 2003), uses the delightful image of "the ambidextrous God of the Bible." (See the Endnotes for the reference and full discussion.) While God's left hand provides structure for society—think of parenthood, government, school, organizations—it is people's overstepping of these boundaries that causes distress among communities as they feel the consequences of these breaches. If, like me, you have that sinking feeling in your stomach while driving "a bit over the speed limit" and see the flashing red, white, and blue lights directly in the rearview mirror, you are experiencing God's left hand.

As a representative of what the prophets said, we look first at Hosea. Hosea is commanded to marry a *"wife of whoredom"* (Hosea 1:2), thus symbolizing the adulterous relationship Israel had with its surrounding culture. Hosea is commanded to name his son *Jezreel* (God sows), for Yahweh would *"punish the house of Jehu for the blood of Jezreel, and…will put an end to the kingdom of the houses of Israel"* (Hosea 1:4). The prophet is commanded to name is daughter *Lo-ruhamah* (not pitied), for *"(Yahweh) will no longer have pity on the house of Israel or forgive them"* (Hosea 1:6). Yet God offers hope for the future, in that God will reestablish the loving, non-adulterous relationship with Israel:

> *Therefore, I will now allure her, and bring her into the wilderness, and speak tenderly to her. From there I will give her, her vineyards and make the Valley of Achor a door of hope. There she shall respond as in the days of her youth, as at the time when she came out of the land of Egypt. On that day, says the LORD, you will call me, "My husband," and no longer will you call me, "My Baal." For I will remove the names of the Baals from her mouth, and they shall be mentioned by name no more. I will make for you a covenant on that day with the wild animals, the birds of the air, and the creeping things of the ground; and I will abolish the bow, the sword, and war from the land; and I will make you*

> *lie down in safety. And I will take you for my wife*
> *forever; I will take you for my wife in righteousness*
> *and in justice, in steadfast love, and in mercy. I will*
> *take you for my wife in faithfulness; and you shall*
> *know the* LORD. (Hosea 2:14–20)

Perhaps the culmination of God's intense love for God's people is expressed in Hosea 11, in which God acknowledges the faithlessness of both Israel and Judah, and yet despite their despicable actions, God exposes the divine heart of unconditional love:

> *When Israel was a child, I loved him, and out*
> *of Egypt I called my son. The more I called them, the*
> *more they went from me; they kept sacrificing to the*
> *Baals, and offering incense to idols...*
> *How can I give you up, Ephraim? How can*
> *I hand you over, O Israel? How can I make you*
> *like Admah: How can I treat you like Zeboiim? My*
> *heart recoils within me; my compassion grows warm*
> *and tender. I will not execute my fierce anger; I will*
> *not again destroy Ephraim; for I am God and no*
> *mortal, the Holy One in your midst, and I will not*
> *come in wrath.* (Hosea 11:1–2, 8–9)

The historical record is different, however; indeed, Israel, the northern kingdom, ceased to exist after the Assyrians invaded and practiced ethnic cleansing. How can we reconcile God's promise of *"I will not again destroy Ephraim"* with the merciless advance of Assyrian armies? Does what happened in history observed purely objectively cancel out God's Word?

The sad reality is that many people *do* prefer a God who punishes severely, and I posit that the Scriptures of the Old Testament that speak God's command for total destruction of cities and peoples is actually a reflection of *our* desire, not God's.

The colonial preacher Jonathan Edward's classic 1742 sermon *"Sinners in the Hands of an Angry God"* is the result of such a theology that is really short on grace, and Edwards is excoriating his own congregation of the faithful! But this is what humanity does so well:

> *The God that holds you over the pit of hell, much as one holds a spider, or some loathsome insect over the fire, abhors you and is dreadfully provoked: his wrath towards you burns like fire; he looks upon you as worthy of nothing else, but to be cast into the fire; he is of purer eyes than to bear to have you in his sight; you are ten thousand times more abominable in his eyes, than the most hateful venomous serpent is in ours. You have offended him infinitely more than ever a stubborn rebel did his prince; and yet it is nothing but his hand that holds you from falling into the fire every moment. It is to be ascribed to nothing else, that you did not go to hell the last night; that you was suffered to awake again in this world, after you closed your eyes to sleep. And there is no other reason to be given, why you have not dropped into hell since you arose in the morning, but that God's hand has held you up. There is no other reason to be given why you have not gone to hell, since you have sat here in the house of God, provoking his pure eyes by your sinful wicked manner of attending his solemn worship. Yea, there is nothing else that is to be given as a reason why you do not this very moment drop down into hell.*

Edwards is keeping good company with so many of the prophetic statements found in the Hebrew Bible. For example, in Jeremiah 16, the prophet responds to the question that people have about God's judgment:

> *It is because your ancestors have forsaken me, says the LORD, and have gone after other gods and have served and worshiped them, and have forsaken*

me and have not kept my law; and because you have behaved worse than your ancestors, for here you are, every one of you, following your stubborn evil will, refusing to listen to me. Therefore, I will hurl you out of this land into a land that neither you nor your ancestors have known, and there you shall serve other gods day and night, for I will show you no favor. (Jeremiah 16:11–13)

Casting Far and Wide—for What?

Jeremiah speaks further God's words:

> *I am now sending for many fishermen, says the* LORD, *and they shall catch them; and afterward I will send for many hunters, and they shall hunt them from every mountain and every hill, and out of the clefts of the rocks. For my eyes are on all their ways; they are not hidden from my presence, nor is their iniquity concealed from my sight.* (Jeremiah 16:16–17)

The fishermen (and hunters) are sent out for the purpose of judgment and punishment, sent to afflict the comfortable people who seem to have no clue as to why they are set to undergo such wrath.

Even Jesus used the image of fishing for people. Upon calling his disciples, he said to them, in Mark's gospel, *"Follow me and I will make you fish for people"* (Mark 1:17). And again in Matthew 4, he uses the image of fishing for people. When the former fishermen—now called to be fishermen!—follow him, *"Jesus went throughout Galilee, teaching in their synagogues and proclaiming the good news of the kingdom and curing every disease and every sickness among the people"* (Matthew 4:23).

What Jesus does is reinterpret the function and purpose of God's fishermen; it is now not for the purpose of *judgment*, as in Jeremiah, but rather to *proclaim the good news of God's kingdom come among people*—a kingdom marked by grace, mercy, compassion, and acted out in the very person of Jesus.

It's a striking reversal of the ancient biblical image and can also keep us honest in what kind of a God we are proclaiming and witnessing to. It challenges our motivation as to what the purpose of our evangelism programs is—to build up the congregation for survival's sake or to proclaim God's good news in Jesus.

YOU *REALLY* WANT A KING?

But to return to Jeremiah… Kings in the ancient Near East were considered to be the shepherds of their people, being anointed as the son of God (see Psalm 2) and entrusted with messiahship, in order to allow the people to flourish as God intended. Yet over time the Lord God expressed great divine frustration with kingship, and said in Jeremiah 23:

> *"Woe to the shepherds who destroy and scatter the sheep of my pasture!" says the LORD. "Therefore," thus says the LORD, "the God of Israel, concerning the shepherds who shepherd my people: It is you who have scattered my flock, and have driven them away, and you have not attended to them. So I will attend to you for your evil doings," says the LORD. "Then I myself will gather the remnant of my flock out of all the lands where I have driven them, and I will bring them back to their fold, and they shall be fruitful and multiply. I will raise up shepherds over them who will shepherd them, and they shall not fear any longer, or be dismayed, nor shall any be missing," says the LORD.*
>
> *"The days are surely coming," says the LORD, "when I will raise up for David a righteous Branch, and he shall reign as king and deal wisely, and shall execute justice and righteousness in the land. In his days Judah will be saved and Israel will live in safety. And this is the name by which he will be*

called: 'The Lord is our righteousness.'" (Jeremiah 23:1–7)

Notice the preponderance of the pronoun *I*. Not depending on flawed humanity, God says, *"I, I myself"* (emphatic in Hebrew) will give the gift of righteous kings, who will execute God's gracious will so that fear will not dominate the lives of the people, and the lost will be found and reintegrated into community. In addition, the Righteous Branch will be the epitome of God's infinite and all-encompassing care for the people of God. When the idea of The Day of the Lord is carried through Scripture, one sees that the cataclysmic time of God's vengeance and recompense is tempered by hope for the future.

Note has been made of the dire words of the prophets when they considered what The Day would mean. The words of Joel 2:1–2a: *"Blow the trumpet in Zion; sound the alarm on my holy mountain! Let all the inhabitants of the land tremble, for the day of the Lord is coming, it is near—a day of darkness and gloom, a day of clouds and thick darkness!"* are expanded further in the quote from Amos 8:9 that was already mentioned: *"On that day, says the Lord God, I will make the sun go down at noon, and darken the earth in broad daylight."*

The inbreaking of Yahweh would be accompanied by unmistakably dramatic natural phenomena, much as Yahweh demonstrated Yahweh's presence on Mt. Sinai during the times of wandering in the wilderness after the Exodus.

Good Friday

Each of the synoptics (Matthew, Mark, and Luke) reports the natural phenomena on Good Friday as Jesus hangs on the cross:

> *From noon on, darkness came over the whole land until three in the afternoon.* (Some manuscripts report darkness over the whole earth.) (Matthew 27:45)

> *When it was noon, darkness came over the whole land (earth) until three in the afternoon.* (Mark 15:33)

> *It was now about noon, and darkness came over the whole land (earth) until three in the afternoon, while the sun's light failed; and the curtain of the temple was torn in two.* (Luke 23:44–45)

One can see in these natural phenomena the visionary words of the prophets Joel and Amos, in that *God has now acted decisively on behalf of sinful humanity.* God has come among humanity in the person of Jesus of Nazareth and demonstrates God's gracious love on the cross of suffering and shame. In other words, the long-desired and hoped-for Day of the Lord took place in Jerusalem during the governorship of Pontius Pilate during a Roman occupation. Yes, the worldly and religious powers held sway over Jesus and see in his death on the cross the removal of a troublesome Jew, a rabbi who taught love and acceptance to their dismay. But that was overturned on the third day.

The story of Good Friday is a continuation of how God chooses to reveal his godself to us. Even Jesus, facing arrest in the Garden of Gethsemane, indicated that he could have called upon the Father to send the heavenly hosts to rescue him from his fate: "*Do you think that I cannot appeal to my Father, and he will at once send me more than twelve legions of angels*" (Matthew 26:53)?

But Jesus indicated that the Scriptures must be fulfilled, and the obedience that marked his faith resulted in his death on the cross. Yet even undergoing one of the cruelest deaths humanity has invented, his words from the cross are words of grace and mercy, directed not only to those who put him to death but also to us all: "*Father, forgive them, for they do not know what they are doing*" (Luke 23:34).

Timeless Words

These words are spoken in a moment of grand, divine *kairos*. The Koiné of the Greek New Testament uses two words for time: *chronos* and *kairos*.

Our English word *chronological* is based on the first word, and it refers naturally to the measured march of time: seconds, minutes, hours, days, weeks, and so on. So Jesus died on a Friday during the governorship of Pontius Pilate, and although the exact date and year are approximate, the day is "measurable."

Kairos, on the other hand, refers to "God's time," which is not bound by time and space, and therefore the words that the dying Jesus speaks reach out to us, too, almost two millennia removed from the historic event on Good Friday. The forgiveness the Son implored the Father to grant us is the wellspring of the forgiveness we hear during the Confession of Sins prior to the Service of worship proper:

> *Almighty God, in his mercy, has given his Son to die for us and, for his sake, forgives us all our sins. As a called and ordained minister of the Church of Christ, and by his authority, I therefore declare to you the entire forgiveness of all your sins, in the name of the Father, and of the Son, and of the Holy Spirit. (Lutheran Book of Worship, Brief Order for Confession and Forgiveness)*

Jesus' words are therefore timeless and certainly relevant—and needed!—in every day and age. For humanity still suffers from its brokenness as much today as in the many years past. For we, too, need to hear these words of grace and mercy on a regular basis, not only so that we receive this blessing of forgiveness from the Father, but also importantly, that we practice among our fellow human beings what God so freely gives. The past lives in the present—and the future—as words of *kairos*, sustaining us week in and week out as we struggle to live out our faith. But what about the future? Is there truly hope?

A Scary Future

It is hugely distressing that certain Christian images of the future, supposedly grounded in Scripture, create more angst and fear than offering a secure comfort. Just think of the last book in the New Testament, *The Revelation.* If, as I said earlier, that the purpose of Scripture is to create and/or sustain faith, a terribly misinterpreted *Revelation* does the opposite, in that it scares folks. We are not called to face the future with dread but with confidence: God has secured the future for us, and we are not to doubt this truth.

But unfortunately, pop culture (think of the *Left Behind* series, for example) creates a dramatic, frightening, and unevangelical interpretation of John the Elder's vision. Fundamentalist preaching uses the images of the Revelation to create time lines, tracking this or that politician as the Antichrist and predicting the end of the world as we know it, marked by a stark separation of humanity into two groups: those saved and those condemned.

How to make sense of all this? We return to that most helpful German phrase of *Sitz im Leben. Sitz im Leben* calls us to address exactly what was happening in the lives of the folks who first read/ listened to this book. What were their circumstances? How was John trying to sustain them?

Scholars commonly date the writing of the Revelation to circa AD 95/96, during the reign of the Emperor Domitian. Domitian instituted a particularly nasty persecution against Christians, and John, the Elder to whom the vision is granted, was caught up in the events. He was exiled to the *"island called Patmos because of the word of God and the testimony of Jesus."* He writes to share with fellow believers in Jesus *"the persecution and the kingdom and the patient endurance"* (Revelation 1:9).

So he is writing to those who are feeling the political/societal pressure of not conforming to the expectations and demands of the state. That is what his readers are experiencing. John then goes on to describe out-of-this-world heavenly visions that end with a climactic battle of God versus the dragon/serpent/devil/Satan.

This genre of writing is called *apocalyptic*, from the Greek ἀποκάλυψις, *revelation* or *disclosure*. Apocalyptic writings arise at a time of extreme circumstances, tremendous pressure on certain groups in society, and are, in and of themselves, "extreme" in the images that are presented. The writer discloses special visions that are granted to him by God for the purpose of strengthening God's people suffering under their present circumstances. So the ultimate purpose of apocalyptic is not to predict the future by doing the math, creating timetables and charts, and attempting to set an absolute date when these things are to take place. Rather, apocalyptic writings address an ongoing situation in the lives of its readers, who are seeking comfort and strength *now*, not some time in the dim future. If one is suffering, one wants relief *now*, and saying that "eventually" relief will come isn't terribly helpful.

This particular style of writing is, however, not unique to the New Testament, for in the Hebrew Bible, the book of Daniel has the same elements; indeed, much of *Daniel's* vivid imagery is incorporated in John's visions. What makes this Old Testament book apocalyptic?

Daniel is set during the time of the Babylonian Exile of the sixth century BC, after the Babylonians had sacked Jerusalem, destroyed the First Temple, and carted off many of the Jerusalemites. (Psalm 137, mentioned earlier, dates from this time.) It contains the well-known stories of Daniel in the lion's den; Shadrach, Meshach, and Abednego in the fiery furnace; the handwriting on the wall; and a great conflict of the nations and heavenly powers.

As a book of Apocalyptic, Daniel's purpose is to strengthen God's people at a time of crisis, much like the Revelation. In other words, Daniel looks *back* to a time when God came to the aid of the

Jews living in Babylon. The message is clear: just as God helped in the past, so too will God intervene and help those who are experiencing distress, persecution, and anxiety in their own lives.

Therefore, Daniel, with a fair amount of certainly, can be dated to a specific time in Jerusalem's history: sometime between 167 and 164 BC the Seleucid King Antiochus IV Epiphanes took control of the city. Antiochus desecrated the temple, most likely by installing a Greek pagan altar, and was finally driven out by the Maccabees, a Jewish clan dedicated to the restoration of the sacrificial system after the temple was cleansed from its defilement. (The Jewish celebration of Hannukah is based upon this time in history and marks the return of proper worship in the Jerusalem temple.)

Even the Synoptic Gospel accounts relate what is called a "little apocalypse" because Jesus speaks about the end times (*eschatology.*) While speaking about the end times in Matthew 24, he reassures his listeners that God has already won the victory over evil forces and that *"heaven and earth will pass away, but my words will not pass away"* (Matthew 24:35).

In Mark 13, he encourages his followers to *"keep awake"* at all times (verse 35) because we can rest assured that God will indeed come. And perhaps Luke 21:28 offers the greatest hope: *"Stand up and raise your heads, because your redemption is drawing near."*

So the apocalyptic passages in the gospel accounts acknowledge that, yes, the world is fraught with turmoil and danger, but God has overcome this chaos and gives us victory over worldly evils.

Thus, apocalyptic literature (primarily Daniel and the Revelation in the Bible) addresses the stresses that God's people were feeling, with the intent of strengthening their trust in God to come to their aid. And if followers of Christ were martyred, they would still share in Jesus' victory over death, the grave, and Hades. That's the promise.

John's images can be frightening if interpreted in such a manner as to predict a terrible scenario at the end of time. Such interpretations of *eschatology* (considering the *last days*) do more to frighten people instead of comforting them in the face of adversity.

As an aside, the figure of the Antichrist does not appear in the Revelation even though many readers claim to find that figure there.

Technically speaking, the Antichrist—the term is used only in the letters of John—refers to those former members of a Christian community who deny the incarnation of Jesus and have left or were put out of the congregation. So the Antichrist arises from *within* Christianity, from *within* congregations. Historically, however, the Antichrist title is given to all sorts of nasty people; even Luther used the term to describe the pope in Rome during his acrimonious debate with the papacy. As the conflict with Rome became irreparable, Luther grew more strident in his attacks on the papacy. As an example, his earliest catechisms commonly used woodcuts to portray various biblical scenes. As early woodcut shows a crocodilian figure emerging from water with a kingly crown on its head. In later editions, this crown eventually morphed into the papal tiara, thus in a graphic manner tying the pope to the enemies of Christ in the Revelation.

But in spite of the terrifying and scary scenarios that John reports, the ultimate purpose of his writing is to give hope—hope that even if (in his context) the Roman Empire has become a terrifying, devouring beast, it is God through the Crucified One who conquers. Not with arms but rather with the Word. Armed with this Word, the Lamb who was slain overcomes God's adversaries. And because the victory of the Lamb who was slain is a moment in *kairos*, God's time, the Crucified and Risen One comes even to each and every one of us in every age in our own times of distress. Those who follow Jesus and call him Lord share in God's victory.

THE LAMB WHO WAS SLAIN

Worthy is the Lamb who was slaughtered to receive power and wealth and wisdom and might and honor and glory and blessing!

—Revelation 5:12

Although the terror of the Revelation images is yet to come in John of Patmos' vision, the text makes clear that it is the Crucified and Risen One, Jesus of Nazareth, who has conquered the powers that line up to dethrone God—not by violence but by the Word of God, his two-edged sword. Combining images from both Daniel and Zechariah, Jesus is introduced as the one who was crucified and slain: "*Look! He is coming with the clouds; every eye will see him, even those who pierced him; and on his account all the tribes of the earth will wail*" (Revelation 1:7).

Jesus' triumph related in text and hymnody is an integral part of the Christian liturgy, and we do well to remember that it is Christ *crucified* who is victorious. Not as an armed warrior but rather as the Lamb who was slain and who was granted life again by the Father.

WORTHY IS CHRIST, THE LAMB WHO WAS SLAIN

The image of Jesus as a Lamb is one of the earliest depictions of the Christ and is naturally based upon Scripture. Twice in St. John chapter 1, John the Baptist recognizes Jesus for who he is: "*Here is the Lamb of God who takes away the sin of the world*" and "*Look, here is the Lamb of God*" (John 1:29, 36).

There is an extensive ancient history of sacrifice in the Hebrew Bible, which we touched upon briefly when contemplating the sacrifice of Isaac in Genesis 22. Isaac was spared at the last moment, and a ram substituted in his place. Worship of Yahweh entailed animal sacrifice, and the unblemished lamb came to define Jesus. The issue was sinfulness, and the expiation of sin came through a change in behavior (heart) and the sacrifice in Israelite worship. The outward act of sacrifice would mirror the inner change so necessary in repentance. So it would be natural to understand the death of the innocent Jesus in terms of Israelite/Jewish worship—only an unblemished animal would be acceptable in the attempt to reconcile with God.

That is, only the perfect sacrifice would satisfy God, and the sinless Jesus does that. Here we touch upon one of the foundational theological motifs of the New Testament: that Jesus died on the cross as the expiation for our sin, the sin of Adam and Eve that has infected all of humanity in all times.

St. Anselm of Canterbury (1033–1109) is one of the foremost theologians of the Western church who developed one of the numerous theories of atonement—at times expressed as *at-one-ment*, the goal being full reconciliation with God. Anselm's take on atonement is called the *Satisfaction Theory* because it is based partially on a legalistic understanding of justice. Affronts to justice must be atoned for, and injustice must be balanced out by an action. As Jesus is the sinless one, his going to the cross is called *supererogatory obedience*—he voluntarily went far beyond the demands of the situation given his credentials as the Son to accomplish what he did for us. For Anselm, God's honor must be satisfied, which happened on the cross. (Another earlier atonement theory that Anselm found insufficient is entitled the *Ransom Theory of Atonement*, which included the devil in its understanding of Jesus' action.) In later centuries, John Calvin stated that Christ suffered the Father's just punishment as a vicarious substitute. (Thanks to *Wikipedia, the Free Encyclopedia*, for its succinct summary of the Satisfaction Theory of Atonement.)

Especially during the Season of Lent do we hear much about atonement. The hymn *"Deep Were His Wounds"* (LBW 100) by William Johnson is one such example:

> *Deep were his wounds, and red,*
> *On cruel Calvary,*
> *As on the cross he bled in bitter agony.*
> *But they, whom sin has wounded sore,*
> *Find healing in the wounds he bore.*
> *He suffered shame and scorn,*
> *And wretched, dire disgrace;*
> *Forsaken and forlorn,*
> *He hung there in our place.*
> *But all who would from sin be free*
> *Look to his cross for victory.* (verses 1, 2)

Paul, in writing to the Romans, touches powerfully upon the idea of atonement, even using the word in his argument concerning God's righteousness:

> *But now, apart from law, the righteousness of*
> *God has been disclosed, and is attested by the law*
> *and the prophets, the righteousness of God through*
> *faith in Jesus Christ for all who believe. For there is*

> *no distinction, since all have sinned and fall short*
> *of the glory of God; they are now justified by his*
> *grace as a gift, through the redemption that is in*
> *Christ Jesus, whom God put forward as a sacrifice*
> *of atonement by his blood, effective through faith.*
> (Romans 3:21–25)

Atonement, whatever theory one clings to, is understandably pervasive in our attempt to "make sense" of what happened in Jerusalem on Good Friday. And while followers of Jesus undoubtedly accept this theology, what does an unbeliever think about this: a God who demands blood? Such thoughts circle back, subtly or not, to the Old Testament God who commanded the destruction of entire cities with no pity extended to the inhabitants, be they male, female, child, or animal.

So how does one reconcile the God of good news, about whom Jesus talked, with various atonement theories? Perhaps a very small detail in John's Gospel can point us in a new direction.

The Seven Last Words of Jesus, sometimes used as a theme in Good Friday worship and preaching, is a conflation of things Jesus said from the cross as recorded in the four gospel accounts.

In John's account of the death of Jesus, he writes:

> *After this, when Jesus knew that all was now*
> *finished, he said (in order to fulfill the Scripture),*
> *"I am thirsty." A jar full of sour wine was standing*
> *there. So they put a sponge full of the wine on a*
> *branch of hyssop and held it to his mouth. When*
> *Jesus had received the wine, he said, "It is finished."*
> *Then he bowed his head and gave up his spirit.*
> (John 19:28–30)

Notice what the sponge is put on. Matthew writes:

> *And about three o'clock Jesus cried with a loud*
> *voice, 'Eli, Eli, lema sabachthani?' that is, 'My God,*

> *my God, why have you forsaken me?' When some*
> *of the bystanders heard it, they said, 'This man is*
> *calling for Elijah.' At once one of them ran and got*
> *a sponge, filled it with sour wine, put it on a stick,*
> *and gave it to him to drink."* Matthew 27:46–48

Notice the difference in how the sponge is offered to Jesus. (Mark also records "stick.") What is an often-overlooked detail in John's gospel is important.

In Exodus 12, God instructs Moses and Aaron as to how they are to prepare the people for the imminent exodus from slavery in Egypt:

> *Then Moses called all the elders of Israel and*
> *said to them, "Go, select lambs for your families,*
> *and slaughter the Passover lamb. Take a bunch*
> *of hyssop, dip it in the blood that is in the basin,*
> *and touch the lintel and the two doorposts with the*
> *blood in the basin. None of you shall go outside the*
> *door of your house until morning. For the* LORD *will*
> *pass through to strike down the Egyptians; when he*
> *sees the blood on the lintel and on the two doorposts,*
> *the* LORD *will pass that door and will not allow the*
> *destroyer to enter your houses to strike you down."*
> (Exodus 12:21–23)

Note the instruction in how the blood is to be daubed on the lintel and the doorposts in order to save those inside: with a bunch of *hyssop*. It is clear that the blood of the lamb saves the people from destruction; and the same image being used in John's account of the crucifixion gives us an understanding of what Jesus' death means aside from a strict atonement parallel.

So where does any one of the atonement theories leave us? I suspect for those who know nothing about the faith, or have turned away from it, any legalistic understanding of Jesus' death on the cross would further alienate those who reject God based on things we have already considered.

Perhaps, instead of thinking in terms of atonement, one ought to consider Jesus' death as the supreme example of the lengths to which God will go to demonstrate unconditional love. In spite of the thought that Jesus was "born to die," we have his own words that he *"came that they may have life and have it abundantly"* (John 10:10).

However we want to understand "abundant life," and I don't mean life measured and defined by materialism and worldly success, one important aspect of it is to be freed from an off-putting understanding of God as the ultimate severe judge, as Jonathan Edwards demonstrates with unforgettable imagery.

Rather, the words of grace and mercy spoken from the cross, *"Father, forgive them,"* create the ultimate invitation to reconcile with God through love, not fear of judgment. Again, it is God's action on the cross which brings healing, and to use the imagery from Exodus, it is Jesus' blood which effects this.

From Thence He Shall Come to Judge the Quick and the Dead

The above sentence is taken from an older version of the Apostles' Creed (Lutheran *Service Book and Hymnal,* 1956.) It refers to the ultimate hope for the Christian: that in due time, *God's* time, our Lord Jesus will return to earth, coming down from heaven in an awesome display of divine power and might to establish permanently the Kingdom of God. All three of the ecumenical creeds (The Nicene, Apostles', and Athanasian) confess this return of Jesus.

In practical terms, this return of Jesus is called the Second Coming.

The New Testament, however, uses a different term to describe this event. The word is παρουσία, transliterated *parousia*. It is a technical term that originates in ancient customs concerning the king or emperor of the day. Especially Roman emperors, when they travelled around the empire, intentionally made a big deal of their coming. Drums, horns, troops, banners, processions demonstrating the wealth and irresistible might of the empire—for political reasons, this was a smart way to notify the populace, "don't mess with Rome."

This type of performance has, of course, fallen mostly by the wayside in today's day and age, and even the convoluted preparations to have the president of the United States stop unannounced and get a Burger King lunch pale in comparison to what royalty did. Perhaps the British come closest to these *parousia*-style theatrics on the occasional appearance of the monarch in parliament; the queen or king is decked out with robes, crown, and such. The trappings of the Roman emperor or the British monarch are meant to display the "heavy weight" of the state in the person who personifies it. Perhaps the closest citizens of the United States might come to that state of affairs is Inauguration Day for the newly elected president.

In any case, *parousia* means that the person or individual is revealed for who he or she is in glory. Such is our expectation of the *parousia* of Jesus. But the term doesn't refer to a *coming* so much as it refers to the *revelation* of that person's royal status if we use the image of king, queen, or emperor. So what we are saying is that at the end of time, Jesus will be shown for who he truly is: King of kings, and Lord of lords.

But what about the meantime? Where is he now? What if we were to say he is present even now with us? That might sound like, "yeah, right, just look at the mess the world is in. Some King Jesus."

Toward the end of Matthew's gospel, Jesus, sitting on the Mount of Olives prior to Thursday's meal, his arrest, and the events of Good Friday, is concluding his public ministry and teaching. He tells the "Parable of the Sheep and Goats":

> *When the Son of Man comes in his glory, and all the angels with him, then he will sit on the throne of his glory. All the nations will be gathered before him, and he will separate people one from another as a shepherd separates the sheep from the goats, and he will put the sheep at his right hand, and the goats at the left. Then the king will say to those at his right hand, "Come, you that are blessed by my Father, inherit the kingdom prepared for you from the foundation of the world; for I was hungry, and you gave me food, I was thirsty and you gave me something to drink, I was a stranger and you wel-comed me. I was naked and you gave me clothing, I was sick and you took care of me, I was in prison and you visited me."* (Matthew 25:31–36)

And upon the question of the righteous, asking when they had ministered to the Son of Man, the response is this: *"Truly I tell you, just as you did it to one of the least of these who are members of my family, you did it to me"* (Matthew 25:40.)

What this means is that Jesus, as part of the Holy Trinity, as God, is not ensconced in heaven, waiting for the blast of the trumpet to set the last things in motion. Rather, Jesus is here right now, with us right now. Not in the person of high rank, not in the wealthy, those of political influence—but in the poor, the vulnerable, the downtrodden, the wounded, the victims of prejudice.

Jesus identifies with the least of the least at this point in time because he still comes to us as the *crucified* yet risen Lord. Yes, he rose on Easter as the result of God raising him from the grave, and he appeared to the disciples multiple times. Even so, he is identified as Jesus by the wounds he still bears: To Thomas, he said, *"Put your finger here and see my hands. Reach out your hands and put it in my side"* (John 20:27).

We are called to recognize Jesus the Risen One by the wounds he still bears. For it is in the *crucified* Jesus that we not only recognize him today but also see opened for us the very heart of God, a God of infinite compassion, mercy, forgiveness, and welcome. That is why Paul, in writing to the Corinthians, wrote that the followers of Jesus *"proclaim Christ crucified, a stumbling block to Jews and foolishness to Gentiles, but to those who are the called, both Jews and Greeks, Christ the power of God and the wisdom of God. For God's foolishness is wiser than human wisdom, and God's weakness is stronger than human strength"* (1 Corinthians 1:23–25).

So God opens God's heart on the cross and, still bearing wounds in Jesus, calls us to serve the neighbor in need with *agape* love. For our fellow neighbors all bear wounds—as we do too!—and by these wounds we recognize Christ in them. Therefore, the *parousia* of our Lord Jesus Christ not only gives us hope for the future when Jesus is revealed in all his kingly glory and recreates the cosmos. It has practical consequences for each and every Christian because, as Jesus said, we will always have the poor—and the downtrodden, the victims of society, the ill, the hungry, the homeless—with us until he is revealed in power and glory. This is why it is so critical that congregations participate in social ministry projects and also advocate for those who have little or no voice. It becomes a *theological* issue: does the congregation share in Jesus' suffering in this world right now or not? If yes, our good works do not bring in the kingdom any sooner—they point to it but do not cause God to adjust God's timetable. Rather, not doing good works has a congregation run the risk of the risen Jesus, who commanded John of Patmos to write this to the church in Ephesus, chiding it:

> *But I have this against you, that you have abandoned the love you had at first. Remember, then from what you have fallen; repent, and do the works you did at first. If not, I will come to you and remove your lampstand from its place, unless you repent.* (Revelation 2:4–5)

The caution is against abandoning *agape*, the serving love of God demonstrated in sending Jesus to us. So we have been given the grace of purpose and meaning as we await the *parousia* of our Lord.

Perhaps that is why the Aramaic word used by Paul in 1 Corinthians 16:22 is so appropriate for all of us. In his closing remarks, he cries out, "*Our Lord, come!*" The original word is *maranatha*, usually translated as above. However, it can also mean "*Our Lord has come!*" And that is exactly where we are as Christians: *Schon, noch nicht*—German words meaning *already, not yet*. The victory over sin, death, and the devil has already been won. The Kingdom of God (the rule of God) is already here. But not yet in its fullness. That is the great tension found in the lives of Christians. That is why we are, as Luther taught, both saint and sinner at the same time. We know we have been saved by the death of Jesus, and yet we still struggle in daily life.

CONCLUSION

This brief survey is obviously not meant to be an all-encompassing study of the Bible. Further study of the Scriptures is always recommended as differing interpretations often help one make the message of Scripture an integral part of one's life as we struggle with God's Word.

In attempting to resolve my own questions about God's interactions with humanity, I have come to several conclusions (which still raise more questions).

First we cannot fully know the Holy One. To claim to know God fully is to lay a claim on God, in that God must therefore act and respond according to one's understanding of who God is. God is the *Holy One*, the one who is sovereign and who owes us *nothing*. Consider God's forceful words to Job:

> *Where were you when I laid the foundation of the earth? Tell me, if you have understanding. Who determined its measurements—surely you know! Or who stretched the line upon it? On what were its bases sunk, or who laid its cornerstone when the morning stars sang together, and all the heavenly beings shouted for joy?"* (Job 38:4–7)

God is God, and God acts in freedom and does not need to justify divine ways. Even the divine name of Yahweh protects, in a way, the mystery and inscrutability of who God exactly is; while The Name is frequently translated as *I AM WHO I AM* when Moses encounters God on Sinai in Exodus 3, other possible translations are given in the footnote to verse 14: "*I AM WHAT I AM* or "*I WILL BE WHAT I WILL BE.*"

God acts in freedom, and oftentimes, we cannot fathom why. But we cannot lay claim to understanding God's mind. How does this work out? "*Now the LORD said to Abram, 'Go from your country and your kindred and your father's house to the land that I will show you*" (Genesis 12:1).

There is no reason given why Yahweh chose Abram because even if Abram had faith (trust), Abram was still a flawed individual as all of us are. Simply said, God chose Abram. Period. Thus does Yahweh act in freedom. To try and figure out why God granted humanity free will, as another example, is to lose oneself in an endless discussion/debate because we cannot, this side of eternity, find a satisfactory answer to the source of Adam and Eve's pride. It's simply who we are and, recognizing the story of the Garden of Eden as *descriptive* of how we act and offers the *consequences* of our actions and attitudes, puts a different perspective on who God is.

Secondly God has chosen to reveal what we need to know about God in the face of the divine mystery: what gives us life, what sustains us, what is necessary for all of humanity's interactions with one another. What is revealed? A heart of infinite love, compassion, and mercy. This is the most essential and necessary knowledge for us as people who have faith/trust. Some who have had near-death experiences claim to have experienced such a depth of love and acceptance that they can't even articulate it well. I like to think they have had not a near-death experience but a full-life experience in their encounter with the divine. This is who God is, and that, perhaps, is all we really need to know this side of eternity.

Thirdly biblical exhortations to live in the light of God display a tremendous tension between morality and ethics. Morality can degenerate into an us/them tug-of-war and can easily descend into an either/or way of approaching very complicated issues in life. Ethics, on the other hand, is the battleground between what is right/just and what is good. While morality can end up as good/bad or right/wrong ways of acting out our humanity, the ethical choice we must make take into consideration the fact that oftentimes there is no sinless answer to a question. *If* Jesus was 100 percent human, he was also faced with these very human choices. How did he navigate life when he had to make a choice between what was bad and worse, rather than simply right and wrong? We don't know, of course, but the church has proclaimed him sinless, which, from an *ethical* point of view, allows even Jesus grace when faced with a lose-lose situation. I can't for a minute think that Jesus levitated above the messy nitty-gritty of life but was involved in all of life's complicated situations.

Fourthly the texts that contain God's command of violence toward others are, in my opinion, texts that reflect humanity's wishful thinking; it's easier to blame God for the brutality of the conquest than it is to admit that the process of settling Canaan was brutal, Israel not sparing infants, women, and domestic animals. These texts are part of the biblical record and cannot and should not be ignored, even if they are nonstarters for Sunday worship lessons. Otherwise, it is extremely difficult to reconcile this aspect of God with the God of John 3:16. God loved the entire cosmos, which in John's gospel account are those who oppose God and God's gracious ways. But the conquest is an integral part of the struggle to establish a people dedicated to be the blessing God created and then wants to share blessing with the rest of the world. If the historical details of battles and justification for them have been massaged for the record, these details are still subservient to the thread that runs through Scripture: the call to be a blessing.

Fifthly the future of many congregations is fraught with anxiety due to the mass departure of the population from local parishes. Growing up in the 1950s, "everyone" went to church on Sunday (not true because many in my neighborhood didn't attend at all). Denominations grew astronomically as the postwar generation got its footing in an increasingly materialistic and modernizing society. Building programs flourished, and now, sixty to seventy years later, these same parishes are either on life support or closed permanently through dissolution or merger.

I received a transistor radio in 1958 (first song I heard, Sheb Wooley's "*The Purple People Eater*"), and that technology was something else. Landlines (one phone at the bottom of the steps, black, rotary, party line), three TV channels, the national anthem used as a sign-off at midnight. There was more "time" to be part of a congregation because there weren't as many options for a social life. However, my generation would most assuredly likely have enthusiastically embraced twenty-first century technology back in the day and, therefore, also most likely would have chosen to distance itself from the Church, much as a good percent of the population does today. It's not so much hostility on the part of a large number of folks as it is indifference. But that's not new by any means. There has always been tension between how we live in the world and how we live in God's kingdom. There is a waxing and waning of faith. It's biblical—"*The LORD will not do good, nor will he do harm*" (Zephaniah 1:12). It's *indifference* to the good news that is so disturbing.

Churches that stress justification (God's action) rather than sanctification (our action) seem to be struggling more. Again, grace is still a hard sell for many people. Yet it would be misplaced energy to think that churches must come up with something to "sell" themselves to the public. Rather, our call is to remain true to the gospel—the good news of God's coming among us, particularly in the person of Jesus of Nazareth—and acting out that good news with caring for the vulnerable, the hungry, the homeless, and at the same time, challenging those structures that allow these things to be a reality, especially in wealthy nations.

Jesus promised to be with his followers until the end of the age, and perhaps the church needs to examine how and why it clings to traditional structures, even when it senses they don't work anymore. The call to be faithful to the gospel is what will determine the future shape of congregations, and so there is great flexibility in how that will come about. In my Lutheran tradition, unity is found not in copying how everyone else is doing it but rather in communicating the pure gospel and administering the sacraments. That freedom to find one's own way in strategic ministries allows lay and professional leaders to use their imaginations to convey the good news.

Sixthly the rise of Christian nationalism is of great concern because it stresses not the gospel but human attempts to create the Kingdom of God on earth. Some of my own ancestors left England in colonial times due to religious persecution, eventually found their way to the New World, and created communities, which in turn, ostracized others who didn't conform. While it's tempting to many to legislate a nation where one faith dominates the public square, it's better to remember what Isaiah said in a passage often read on Christmas Eve when talking about the future:

> *For a child has been born for us, a son given to us; authority rests upon his shoulders; and he is named Wonderful Counselor, Mighty God, Everlasting Father, Prince of Peace. His authority shall grow continually, and there shall be endless peace for the throne of David and his kingdom. He will establish and uphold it with justice and with righteousness, from this time onward and forever-more.* The zeal of the LORD of hosts will do this *(my emphasis).* (Isaiah 9:6–7)

The LORD of hosts is the one who will create the kingdom on earth, not the legislative attempts of people. We are called to trust that vision, even while advocating for the vulnerable and working out the call to be a blessing to others. Our good works do not create the everlasting kingdom on earth but point to it and are meant to give hope to those who suffer. Plus, there is the great danger that the faith is used by political figures for their own benefit.

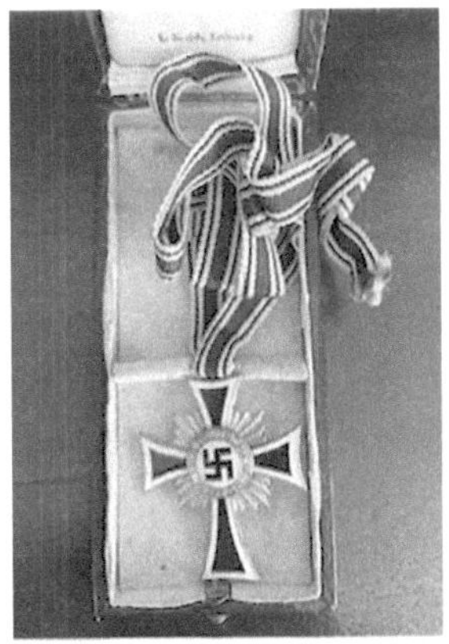

What stands out the most when you first look at the above picture?

The swastika. It dominates the cross as it was meant to. This medal is called a "Mother's Cross" and was awarded by the Nazi party to Aryan women only who had given birth. Depending on the number of children produced, one could receive a bronze, silver, or gold Mother's Cross. (This one was awarded to my great-grandmother in 1938; she had given birth to at least eight children of record, so she was awarded the grand prize, the gold cross.) The intent was to build up the pure German population by encouraging childbirth. And if a mother was found later on to have some non-Aryan blood, the party would demand the cross back. Nazis went to great lengths to denigrate Christianity, and the fact that much of the population of Germany went along with this points out the danger of the state interfering with the Church or any religion, as a matter of fact.

This does not, however, mean that believers are to separate what Luther called the two kingdoms—the kingdom of Caesar and the kingdom of God. Daily life requires all of us to participate actively in the world regardless of where one lives. That means we are to bring our faith to bear on how society is working. But what about *Render to Caesar*? Doesn't this mean that there is indeed a separation between the two kingdoms? Don't we live in God's kingdom on Sunday and then in Caesar's for the rest of the week?

"*'Show me a denarius. Whose head and title does it bear?' They said, 'The emperor's.' He said to them, 'Then give to the emperor the things that are the emperor's and to God the things that are God's'*" (Luke 20:24–25).

There it is, the separation of the two kingdoms. But is it? Would Jesus actually command one to a strict lifestyle of pigeonholing important public issues? Isn't he the one who commands us to bring our faith to bear upon society?

Perhaps the problem with understanding *Render to Caesar* as a command is that it just might not be a command. It goes back to the Greek of the New Testament. Grammatically, statements of fact have verb forms in what is called present active indicative. Commands are known as imperatives, and the translators of this New Testament passage traditionally have chosen to understand *render* as an imperative, a command.

However, in Greek the imperative form (ἀπόδοτε) is the same as the present active indicative, the statement form (ἀπόδοτε). Thus, if we follow this argument, what Jesus is saying to the scribes and the chief priests who were trying to trap him is this: You (All of you, plural) separate life into two distinct arenas. He is turning back on them their hypocrisy in being "religious" when convenient and being loyal citizens when convenient. But Jesus is ahead of them; the fact that they can produce a coin with a pagan (the emperor) on it while on the sacred temple grounds demonstrates their hypocrisy. So rather than build a wall between the two kingdoms, a daily flowing back and forth between the two is a more realistic and faith-oriented posture for Christians, similar to a Möbius strip. And therefore, yes, we are to bring our faith into the voting booth as we discern which candidate will promote policies that, among other things, protect the poor, the immigrant, the homeless, those without health insurance, and so on.

The last point I want to make is our approach to the Bible.

Bibliolatry is one of those seminary buzz words that rarely, if ever, makes it into everyday conversation. Simply put, the Bible turns into an idol. The Scriptures are, of course, the written and handed-down record of God's interactions with humanity. We honor the Scriptures, use them as our guide in life, revere them for the stories of how our ancestors in faith responded to their encounter with God. But there is a reason we confess weekly in the creeds that we *believe* in God the Father, God the Son, and God the Holy Spirit—but we don't confess that we believe in the Bible. This is a hair-raising statement to make for many denominations, I understand. As the *Epitome* of the *Formula of Concord* (sixteenth century Reformation writings contained in the Lutheran *Book of Concord*) states:

> *We believe, teach, and confess that the prophetic and apostolic writings of the Old and New Testaments are the only rule and norm according to which all doctrines and teachers alike must be appraised and judged... The Holy Scripture remains the only judge, rule, and norm according*

*to which as the only touchstone all doctrines should
and must be understood as judged as good or evil,
right or wrong.*

I liken the above understanding of the status of the Bible to a child's paddle with a ball attached to a long rubber band. The paddle is the Bible; the ball is our attempts at understanding the divine mystery, whether that be a new teaching, study, sermon preparation, or advocacy in the legislature. When we are "on target," we hit the ball, and it goes far out from the paddle. When we miss the mark, not much happens except entanglement. So it is with the Bible. That is why we believe in a Person (or the Three in One of the Trinity) but not in the Scriptures. They are *witnesses* to God's interaction with humanity and used to regulate our faith life. And that is also why it is critical to understand the context surrounding the Scriptures. God's Word addresses specific contexts, and what was said at one time might not be exactly applicable later on. For example, Hosea was commanded to get married (to a whore, no less!), and yet Jeremiah (chapter 16) was commanded not to get married and not have children. Which one is it if we are to live according to the Bible? Hosea's marriage was to demonstrate the infidelity of Israel, which chased after idols, thus committing adultery with Yahweh. Jeremiah's prohibition against getting married came at a time when severe judgment was to come upon the land (and therefore, as mentioned earlier, the fishers coming after the population for the purpose of punishment). Western society has for the most part moved (at least legally) from considering women as chattel and that social progress is opposed to much of the Bible, the societies in which it was written being extremely patriarchal. However, we are called to live as new creatures in Christ—meaning we are to live in Genesis 1 and 2 and not Genesis 3. Sadly, we delight in ordering our lives after Genesis 3. Much of the Bible that follows chapter 3 is the struggle to return to the harmony, the *shalom* of God's intent for humanity at the beginning of the Bible. That harmony, that *shalom*, the good news of the kingdom of God, was proclaimed and lived out by Jesus in his life, death, and resurrection.

ENDNOTES

Crossings: March 30 2006. "Philip Jenkin's Global Christianity Viewed through Luther's Lenses" by Ed Schroeder.

https://crossings.org/luther-and-world-christianity

Luther's critique of Christendom. The ambidextrous God of the Bible.

The very title of Jenkins' book, The Next Christendom, would cause Luther to raise an eyebrow. He did not think that Christendom—surely not of his day, and unlikely in any other day—was a good thing. In his view Christendom is a nemesis to the Christian Gospel. By definition, he thought, the Gospel never leads to a "-dom" or "-ianity" of any sort. However one might define "Christian world, Christianity, Christendom," Luther was skeptical of any proposal for establishing a Christian general culture, specifically if "the Gospel" was claimed as the cornerstone for it all. His own lived experience in culture-wide "Christian" Europe with its bi-polar ruling ellipse of the Roman Church in symbiosis—sometimes friendly, sometimes not so—with the Holy Roman Empire, had eventually convinced him that such an all-pervasive wall-to-wall Christian culture was at odds with the Gospel—at least in its Latin form in the Europe of his day. How so?

Although God is indeed one, Luther came to understand that God's work in the world is not unitary, technically speaking not sim-plex, but duplex. Recompense and mercy—though patently divine operations—are not synonyms. Following Biblical patterns of God-talk, especially Isaiah & Jeremiah, Paul & John, and the Letter to the Hebrews, Luther came to see God at work in the world in ambidex-trous fashion. God works with the left hand creating and sustaining creation–especially the stop-gap rules-and-regulations needed to pre-serve a sin-fractured world. God works with the right hand redeem-ing [literally, "regaining ownership of"] that same estranged creation with its now actively antagonistic human creatures, and bringing the whole business back "home" and thus back to its own health and wholeness, a.k.a. salvation and righteousness. Not an easy job, even for God. Whereas God's left-hand work –keeping the planets mov-ing, the cycle of seasons on earth, the sunrise, the teeming oceans, the birds and bees, even the flow of human generations–seems effortless for God, the right-hand agenda was costly, very costly, costing God his own beloved Son to bring it to fruition.

For this right-handed work God's promissory covenant, at least as far back as Abraham (maybe even to Noah and Adam) in the Hebrew scriptures, fulfilled in the crucified and risen Messiah, was the foundational scriptural centerpiece. It was God's "Word" as Gospel. For the left hand, the Sinai covenant of old with its deb-it-credit "suum cuique" orderliness and God's on-going "law written in the heart ... accusing and excusing" those who'd never heard of Sinai was the "other" divine word, Law, that animated it all. The medieval merger of an imperial church and a "holy" empire blended what God distinguished. Christendom contradicted the word and work of God. Yes, one and only one God, but from that same God, two distinctly different words, two differing covenants, two different "diakoniai" (agendas), constituting two different creations–old and new. Same one Rex, but two different regimes, so sharply different that when confronting sinners, one constituted a death sentence, the other life that lasts.

That made any totalitarian worldly regimes, even and especially ones that called themselves "holy," suspect. Since an ambidextrous deity was the operations manager, and since the one and only place where God's two regimes intersected was at Christ's crucifixion, in his body on a tree, any Christendom that claimed to unify those two disparate divine operations within itself was out of order. And Christendoms always seek to do that. Luther saw this "in spades" in both church and state–Holy Roman Church, Holy Roman Empire–of his day. Both went beyond their God-given jurisdictions in implementing God's diverse regimes. The churchly institution divinely authorized for God's right-hand work operated unashamedly within the left-hand realm, even applied left-hand coercive rubrics in its own proper churchly agenda, thus violating the non-coercive Gospel at the center of Christ's own mandate: "coercive authority? It shall not be so among you." And the holy Roman empire–from the emperor all the way down to the peasant level in its own secular hierarchy–merely with its claim to holiness, but even worse with its fingers constantly in God's churchly right-hand agenda, was violating its authorization to be about the Father's left-hand business.

So the model of Christendom that prevailed in the 16th century was abusive of the Gospel. Both institutions that constituted the Siamese twins of Medieval Christianity, Empire and Church, by virtue of putting their "hands" where they did not belong, were nemeses to God's right-hand regime of getting sinners forgiven, getting them joined to Christ, and thus becoming the body of Christ, the core definition of what church is. Luther also observed that this confusion of jurisdictions was also the bane of God's left-hand regime. When God's appointed left-handers pursued church politics, they were shirking their duties in caring for the creation.

So is no "Christian society" possible? Well, that all depends. If/when secular authority sticks to its God-given agenda of God's left-hand caring, preserving, equity-justice work, then you do have the matrix for a godly society, though not a "gospelly" society. When left-handers keep their hands off of soteriology, they are doing the right thing. A "Gospelly" society is what the body of Christ is. Right from the start that society has no political or geographical borders, so no one prince can possibly have authority there–by definition. The one and only authority of that body is Christ, the head. There are no secondary rulers in that regime, since every other participant is but a member. It is a very very flat hierarchy–one head, everybody else equal. And even that head is not situated above the members, exercising authority "over" his underlings, but is himself "beneath" them all, serving "and giving his life as a ransom for many."

God's right-hand regime–on earth just as incarnately as the left-hand regime–appears first of all on the divine-human interface (coram deo) where God's mercy trumps God's justice, new creation overtakes preservation, in short, right-hand trumps left-hand. Now comes stage two. From this "pebble" (see below) dropped into the pool of God's left-handed world, the gospelly society called church is created, and from that pebble ripples emanate. God's right-hand regime is replicated over and over again on the human-human interface where these mercy-managed (former) sinners now enact the very same agenda coram ho minibus, their face-to-face interactions with fellow humans. That is the paradigm. For more on this ripple-effect, see below.

But that does not constitute a Christendom. Godly left-handed societies are what all societies are called to be, and in some cases to achieve, even with no reference to God's other "gospelly" right-hand agenda. From what Luther had heard of Suleiman the Magnificent, he thought that Suleiman was operating a godly left-hand regime among the "Turks." And there was no Christic Gospel in his regime. Luther excoriated Suleiman's murderous onslaught against the Holy Roman Empire to extend Islamic faith. That was, of course, an abomination–Suleiman invading soteriology, a violation of his God-given jurisdiction. His right-hand worked wickedly, but his left-hand –mirabile dictu–did not. If he had only stuck to that "secular" this-world calling, he would have been above reproach. Clearly no attempt at a Christendom, just a good, yes, Muslim, ruler exercising his godly vocation.

[The lands in which the Lutheran Reformation prevailed sought to organize public life and church life according to these rubrics. Some did better than others, e.g., electoral Saxony for a while. But here too sin did not cease to blur the edges. It was not a "separation of church and state," but an awareness that faith is a matter of the heart and thus inaccessible to any legislation or coercion, whilst rules and regulations, and coercion if needed, was proper–yes, god-given– in the body politic. Constantinian Christendom makes faith a "you gotta." In left-hand right-hand Lutheranism it was a "you get to, but you don't have to" be a Christ-confessor to be a legal citizen.]

Christendom in Luther's thought cannot escape authority conflicts–at the most fundamental level. Political authority, Caesar's rightful authority, is (the Latin word) imperium, Christ's authority is (also Latin) dominium. Here are the antitheses: authority over vs. authority under; you serve me vs. I serve you; When the crunch comes, you die to preserve my life vs. when the crunch comes, I die to preserve your life. Political and social structures are patterned as imperium–and rightly so. The structure in the body of Christ is only dominium. To live in both at the same time–as all Christians do (but not-yet Christians don't)–brings tension. This tension is fundamental, because the differing divine regimes are at the base. This side of the parousia it is never totally resolved. But it is endurable, even victoriously so–because of the Gospel.

Bibliography

Bible Society, Page H. Kelley, William R. Scott. *Biblia Hebraica Stuttgartensia.* Deutsche Bibelgesellschaft, Stuttgart, 1977.

Edwards, Jonathan. *Sinners in the Hands of an Angry God.* Northampton, Massachusetts, July 8, 1741.

Evangelical Lutheran Church in America. *Service Book and Hymnal.* Augsburg Publishing House, Minneapolis, Minnesota, and Board of Publications, Lutheran Church in America, Philadelphia, Pennsylvania. 1958.

Lutheran Book of Worship. Augsburg Publishing House. Minneapolis and Board of Publications, Lutheran Church in America, Philadelphia, 1978.

Nestle, Eberhard, Erwin Nestle. *Novum Testamentum Graece (Nestle-Aland).* Deutsche Bibelstiftung, Stuttgart, 1979.

Shroeder, Ed. "Luther and World Christianity: Philip Jenkins' Global Christianity Viewed through Luther's Lenses." *The Crossing Community* (March 30, 2006): https://crossings.org/luther-and-world-christianity/.

The Holy Bible. Oxford University Press. 200 Madison Avenue, New York, New York.

Wengert, Timothy J. *The Book of Concord. The Confessions of the Evangelical Lutheran Church.* Translated and edited by Theodore G. Tappert. Fortress Press, Philadelphia, 1959.

Wikipedia. The Free Encyclopedia. "Satisfaction theory of atonement." https://en.wikipedia.org/wiki/Satisfaction_theory_of_atonement.

Scriptural References

About the Author

Richard J. Mauthe is a teacher of Old and New Testaments for the Grand Canyon Synod of the ELCA Diakonia program. He is a former public school teacher in Pennsylvania and a former adjunct faculty member of the Philadelphia Lutheran Seminary (now United Lutheran), teaching and tutoring Hebrew and New Testament Greek. He is a retired member of the clergy in the Evangelical Lutheran Church in America. He and his wife live in the Tucson area in Arizona.